Spinoza and Kabbalah

Originally published in French as
Spinoza et la Kabbale
in *L'Univers Israélite*, Paris, 1863.

ISBN : 978-2-38366-037-8

© 2024
éditions localement transcendantes
Puyméras, France

Elijah Benamozegh

Spinoza and Kabbalah

*Translated, presented and annotated
by* Yehiel Davenne

FOREWORD

Yehiel Davenne

Elijah Benamozegh was an uninvited guest at the philosophers' banquet. Uninvited, unwanted and quite unpolished. Self-taught in western philosophy and modern sciences, at the end of the xix[e] century, he was a stranger in the room of Parisian metaphysical debates. Born in Livorno in 1823 to a family emigrated from Marocco and orphaned from his father at a young age, his first education was done by his maternal uncle, Rabbi Yehuda Coriat, rabbinical judge of Livorno and author of an important kabbalistic work.[i] This first schooling was only Hebraic and included the complete reading of the Zohar. Thus read under the guidance of an authentic traditionist, the Zohar would remain the central reference and metaphysical inspiration of Benamozegh. This first schooling encompassing the vast span of Hebrew culture, which he shared with Spinoza, should have established his competence as a judge of the latter. But his contribution to the question of the true source

---

i. Rabbi Yehuda Coriat [יהודה קורייאט] (Tétuan, 1770 – Livorno, 1846) published *Maor vaShemesh* [מאור ושמש] (Livorno, 1838), a compendium of ancient kabbalistic sources and personal commentaries ; this book is quoted by Rabbi Tzadok haKohen miLublin.

and nature of Spinoza's ontology went almost unnoticed. His article 'Spinoza and Kabbalah', published in 1863 in the very parochial *L'Univers Israélite*, he wrote directly in the long-winded literary French of the period, which he did not entirely master. I have tried to render his slight awkwardness in my English translation, to keep alive the singularity of his voice as it expresses more than a foreign accent – a point of view irreducible to European culture.

That the question of the influence of Kabbalah on Spinoza's ontology should be problematic is in itself a wonder. It never escaped the acuity of careful readers, Leibniz among them. After the most recent research in the field, it has become hardly deniable.[ii] The long (and in many parts lasting) obfuscation of the fact that the starting point of Spinoza's speculation on the absolute unity of ultimate Being and the production of the finite by the infinite lays in the kabbalistic books he owned and read, cannot be explained but by a conspiracy of ignorance and interest. Ignorance might be excused. Kabbalah literature has only started to be translated and studied.

A cursory review of the interests at play is more interesting. Spinoza has long become the private preserve of enlightened Jewish scholars, for whom he is a personal model and a cultural hero. Compared to the subtlety and profundity of the ontological discussions among the kabbalists, Spinoza's simplification posing as rationalism might pale and show itself as a closure of the mind bordering on charlatanism.

Even more curious, is the destiny of Spinoza as Prophet for some radical circles. An alleged Prophet of

---

ii. See Selected Bibliography, page 83.

the multitudes and radical democratic struggle could not be avowed to be, though heretical, a profoundly religious thinker; some inescapable consequences of his system, such as a State enforced religion for the masses, would have to be hidden; and the absolute sterility of Spinozism in the development of positive sciences would have to be kept untold.

But Benamozegh's contribution is a lot more than a landmark in the history of the retrieval of the intellectual background of Spinoza's thinking. Our Italian kabbalist shows here his philosophical acumen in picking up in Spinoza's system the weakest link: the modes infinite, immediate and mediate. The exact status and function of these modes, at the same time individuality and infinity, is an old puzzle in the interpretation of Spinozism. Commentators have stressed Spinoza's own embarrassment when confronted on this question and challenged to give examples of infinite modes. And this issue is to this day the subject of lively debates among philosophers.[iii]

For Benamozegh's philosophical argument to be easier to follow, I have given in the end notes the complete texts he quotes or alludes to in his intricate disquisition.

But Benamozegh's ultimate intention cannot be grasped without an analysis of his polemical strategy. His main goal in publishing this article was clearly to elevate the intellectual status of Kabbalah in the eyes of his audience: to diagnose Spinoza's ontology as an aberration of Kabbalah is both proving that Kabbalah

---

iii. See for example Alain Badiou, « Pour une interprétation nouvelle de la notion d'attribut de l'absolu », conference at Paris 8 University, May 18, 2017.

is an ontology and that Spinoza's language might be used as a tool to formulate the rational exposition of that ontology, or at least to make the point that such a rational exposition is possible.

This move is but a moment in a much wider polemic. Before even pretending to establish the intellectual legitimacy of the Jewish tradition in the eyes of enlightened Europeans, Rabbi Benamozegh had to confront the western European Jewish intellectual and rabbinical establishment on the antiquity and authenticity of Kabbalah itself.

In *La Kabbale et l'origine des dogmes chrétiens* (published posthumously only in 2011!) Benamozegh deploys a complex strategy to establish, mainly for an enlightened Jewish audience, the antiquity and authenticity of Kabbalah. He first demonstrates that the main features of Christian theology (Trinity, Logos theology, Incarnation) are already clearly present in the New Testament and are not a late elaboration by the Church. He then proceeds to prove that these theological tenets cannot be reduced or explained by any Greek philosophical influence, but are absolutely singular and irreducible to any non-Jewish culture, philosophy or religious tradition. He finally shows that they can be compared only to Kabbalah and understood in its light as an aberration by simplification and conflagration of ontological levels. These tenets are therefore witness to the existence among the Jews of the Second Temple period of an unwritten metaphysical and theological tradition of which Kabbalah is the exposition and development.

This line of argument is the exact counterpart of the one expounded here. Christianity and Spinozism as contradictory as they are, are symmetrical aberrations deviating from a deeper inner core.[iv] As teratological models, they are witness to a hidden Truth, infinitely more immense and beautiful.

Elijah Benamozegh was an unapologetic votary of the *philosophia perennis* tradition. He was convinced that Kabbalah, esoteric Hebraism as he calls it, was its most enduring and most encompassing Monument. His project, of which we present here only a small fragment, was vastly more ambitious: the regeneration of a global Jewish philosophy able to recover the lost harmony with the most advanced human sciences.[v]

---

iv. See the Author's important note xv page 38.

v. "(...) *perchè da gran tempo la ortodossia ebraica non entrò a contatto colla progredita scienza umana; e il ristabilire quest'armonia interrotta, in tutte le parti sue* (...)". *Di Dio. Teologia dogmatica e apologetica*, Livorno, 1877, p. 1.

Spinoza and Kabbalah

Elijah Benamozegh

When I recently read, in the *Revue des Deux-Mondes*, Mr. E. Saisset's excellent article on Maimonides and Spinoza,[1] I listened attentively to the voice of the master who had once introduced me, from my early youth, to the understanding of the Dutch philosopher, through the translation of his works, and especially through the lucid and learned introduction where the whole system of Spinoza appears shortened, much better coordinated and a lot more intelligible than in the pretentiously geometric form that the philosopher gave to his thoughts.

Now as then, it was Spinoza and his philosophy, the subject addressed by Mr. Saisset. But I soon realized that it was, not as in his introduction, the core of Spinoza's ideas, but a perhaps more important question — the origin and filiation of the Dutch Jew's system. The greatness of the subject redoubled my attention and I engaged with all the more interest in this interesting reading as I was aware of having glimpsed the interest of this question for a long time, and, if I may add, of having my preferences and my little system on the subject of the debate.

It is Mr. Saisset who teaches us: three systems, three influences compete for the honor of having inspired Spinoza and of having provided him with the main elements of his philosophy. This three contenders are: Maimonides, Descartes and Kabbalah. Descartes was the first to receive the honor of this paternity. His reign, it seems, has lasted peacefully and unchallenged almost to the present day. Yet there was someone who challenged his legitimacy and who thought it necessary to substitute in public opinion for Descartes a happier rival: Maimonides; and this someone is none but the most famous French philosopher of the nineteenth century, Mr. Cousin. It is mainly about this novel opinion that Mr. Saisset takes up the pen to operate, we will not say a restoration, but a rehabilitation of Descartes' paternal rights to Spinoza's philosophy. I do believe that the titles of Maimonides do not stand up to a thorough examination and Mr. Saisset is perfectly right against Mr. Cousin in denying the predominant influence of Maimonides on the system of Spinoza;[i] he is right, especially when he preserves the fragment of truth in this hypothesis, by very judiciously recognizing Maimonides' influence, not in the Metaphysics of Spinoza, but in the Critique and in the Interpretation of the Sacred Books.

Even there, no offense to Mr. Saisset, there were great reservations and a sharp distinction to be made between the criticism of Maimonides and that of

---

i. One could indeed glimpse analogies between the Arabian peripateticism of Maimonides and the aesthetics of Spinoza; but these analogies derive only from the traces that Neo-Platonic philosophy imprinted on medieval Aristotelianism, as it is today firmly established; and thus, far from proving the origin proposed by Mr. Cousin, they serve only to confirm the borrowings made from Kabbalah, which has so many principles in common with Neo-Platonism.

Spinoza. Perhaps they have in common the proclamation of the rights of Reason in the exegesis of Scripture. But the way they understand the exercise of these rights, is nothing less than similar. To ascertain this, it is enough to read chapter VII of the *Theological-Political Treatise*, where Spinoza, after having exposed Maimonides' system, is so intent to fight it. I will say more: if something obviously results from the examination of this chapter and other similar passages, which will be reproduced, it is that if Spinoza does not spare Maimonides and his exegesis, if he condemns the claim to elevate philosophy and philosophers to supreme judges and to make them the criterion of the meaning of the Scriptures, if he mixes with his harsh judgment the most biting irony, exclaiming in this regard: "*Here is a very new authority in the Church, a new species of priests and pontiffs, and certainly it would inspire less veneration than contempt in the vulgar*"; if he anathemizes his method as excessive and reckless to the highest degree, if he concludes, after a long disquisition, that Maimonides' method is absolutely useless, that it must be rejected as useless, dangerous and absurd, he has much more respectful words, I dare to say even sympathetic for what he calls the tradition of the Pharisees. I draw the attention of scholars to this curious phenomenon, which is not one of the smallest indications of what Spinoza owed to this tradition, and which predisposes us to admit the borrowings that, in my opinion, Spinoza made in large numbers to the most secret part of this same tradition called Kabbalah. We have seen how Spinoza allows himself to slander Maimonides and his exegesis. Is he so bitter, so implacable towards the tradition and exegesis of the Pharisees? Far from it. It can be said, almost with certainty, that he feels attraction if not for the truth of their system, at least for its greatness, for its coherence. This is the best he opposes to his disciple Burgh, who after having passed to Catholicism, thought to call Spinoza himself into the bosom of the Church. Burgh shared with Spinoza his amazement at the sight of the antiquity and continuity of the Catholic tradition. Spinoza retorts with the uninterrupted chain and the otherwise venerable antiquity of the Pharisaic tradition:

> You speak of the unanimous consent of so many thousands of men, of the uninterrupted succession of the Church. But all this is the Pharisees' own language. They produce, with a confidence equal to that of the believers of the Roman Church, myriads of witnesses who have no less stubborn firmness than yours, and who report, as if they had seen them, things they have heard said. And, indeed, no one can deny that all heresies came out of their bosom and that the Pharisees remained faithful to themselves for several thousand years, without any constraint and by the force of superstition alone. I'm not talking about their miracles. A thousand people, and I suppose them chatty, would get tired of telling them. But what they pride themselves on most are their martyrs. They brim with them more than any other nation, and each day increases the number of those of their brothers who know how to suffer for their faith with a singular strength of soul. Here I am myself a witness to their sincerity. I saw, among many others, a certain Judah, whom they call the Faithful, who, raising his voice from the bosom of the blazing pyre where he was already thought to be consumed, sang the hymn: *Tibi, Deus, animam meam offero*, and only interrupted this song to breathe his last.[2]

But these are only sympathetic phrases; we have elsewhere on the tradition of the Pharisees a judgment much less severe than that pronounced against Maimonides. After rejecting the system of the latter[ii], he adds:

> If we are now offered the tradition of the Pharisees or the authority of the pontiffs of Rome, we will say that the former does not agree with itself, and as for the latter, it does not rely on sufficiently authentic testimonies, and we have no other reason to reject it; for if Scripture showed us the authority of these pontiffs as clearly as it does that of the pontiffs of the Old Law, it would not matter to us that there were heretical and impious popes, since they were also found among the Hebrews who were not worth more and who seized the pontificate by illegitimate means; which did not prevent them from exercising the supreme power to interpret the law.[3]

Either I am strangely mistaken, or there are two important things to observe here: the first is that Spinoza finds to object to the tradition of the Pharisees only the fault of agreeing with itself. It is a condemnation, if there is any, very lenient, which, in my opinion, cannot be appreciated precisely without bringing it closer to the eternal objection of the Karaites against the Pharisees, that is to say, the divergence of opinions that reigns between them and which forced Maimonides to proclaim a principle that only the mere drive of polemic may have snatched from him, namely, that any question or dissent does not belong to the Sinaitic tradition. Spinoza's objection

---

ii. *Theological-Political Treatise.*

belongs to the stream of these ideas. But what must be deduced from this is that Spinoza does not venture to deny the general existence of a tradition, but only the uniformity of that of the Pharisees.

He even establishes this existence in express terms about the authority of the Roman pontiffs when, after refusing it for lack of sufficiently authentic testimonies (an objection that he is careful not to direct against the tradition of the Pharisees), he adds:

> And we have no other reason to reject it, for if Scripture showed us the authority of these pontiffs as clearly as it does for that of the pontiffs of the Old Law, it would not matter to us that there were heretical and impious popes, since there were also Hebrews who were no better, and who seized the pontificate by illegitimate means; which did not prevent them from exercising the supreme power to interpret the Law.

Either these words make no sense, or they mean that traditional authority was legitimate among all the Hebrew pontiffs, and that Scripture obliged us to obey them without regard to anything other than their ministry, even when they fell into heresy and impiety. This is the opinion of Spinoza openly stated, and it is, singularly, the pure Pharisaic maxim, which sees authority always respectable, even in its unworthy custodians. [iii]

----

iii. Spinoza even followed to a certain extent the maxim of the rabbis, who did not push their claim to believe themselves inviolable even in the case of a flagrant and voluntary alteration of the Law. If any passage of the Talmud seems to display this claim, the prevailing opinion is far from associating itself with it. It can be said that Spinoza is more royalist here than the king.

A part, and the most important part of this tradition, for which Spinoza has only respectful words, is Kabbalah or the theological tradition. Did he know about it? Had he more or less studied it? I don't think there's any serious doubt about that. Spinoza always shows himself covered from head to foot in the armor of Hebrew scholarship. His childhood, his youth, were spent in the study of Hebrew books. Even after his separation from the Synagogue, he did not cease to borrow from them everything that came about his arguments, witness the many Hebrew-Rabbinic quotations that abound in his accounts and on which he relies; witness also the invocation of a peripatetic rabbi to interpret according to its true meaning the thought of Aristotle, and which he opposes to the way of understanding this philosopher according to the writers of his time. This rabbi is Hasdai Crescas, and this is how he expresses himself on his account:

> The demonstration that the ancient disciples of Aristotle gave of the existence of God, here it is, indeed, as I find it in a Jew named Rab Ghasdaj: "Assuming an infinite progress of causes, all things that exist will be caused things. Now, no caused thing exists necessarily by the force of its nature, so there is in nature no being to whose essence it belongs to necessarily exist. But this consequence is absurd, therefore so is the principle". [iv4]

No, it is not possible to deny with any likelihood that Spinoza knew nothing about Kabbalah, even if we were to ignore the passages that attest to the contrary, and which will be discussed later. His

---

iv. *Letters*, vol. II, page 363.

education, his philosophical curiosity, the doctrines and studies that prevailed in his century among the Dutch Israelites, the credit that Kabbalah enjoyed in his time, not only among his co-religionists, but also in the philosophical world itself, where the Platonic scholars of Italy had already preluded the rehabilitation of these doctrines that is beginning to take place today; everything, finally, opposes the hypothesis of ignorance, on the part of Spinoza, of Kabbalistic doctrines.

Did he reject them, as absurd and without weight and authority, in the field of metaphysics? This is what Mr. Saisset seems to insinuate, to whom ignorance also seems incredible in the condition in which Spinoza lived, studied and composed his works. Is it true, as the illustrious critic claims, that Spinoza had nothing but disdain for the religious philosophy of the Hebrews?

It costs us to separate ourselves from our former guide, and we know what weight this dissent imposes on us; but the most intimate conviction obliges us to oppose it with the most formal of denials. I know that Mr. Saisset relies on disdainful expressions that Spinoza himself has uttered and he obviously alludes to these expressions in his article. But Mr. Saisset does not quote them; and although I have with all my power sought the trace of this disdain by patiently rereading all the *Ethics* and *Letters* of Spinoza, and even by going through his other works, I could not find anything that resembled, near or far, this blame, this direct and formal disdain that tilts the judgment of the illustrious critic to the negative side. Was Mr. Saisset mistaken in his recollections? I would not dare to say so; but, in the meantime, I believe that it will be permissible for us not to give decisive weight to this supposed disdain, and to continue, if possible, our research, taking advantage of other elements that have been otherwise well established. Were it even true that Spinoza expressed himself in the manner indicated about Kabbalah, would this decide the question in favor of Mr. Saisset? Would this preclude any borrowing by Spinoza? Do we dare to argue that Spinoza picked up everything in this esoteric tradition he encountered on the way to his studies? Do we think that he went beyond certain supreme principles that we believe he transplanted from Hebrew theology, by sowing and cultivating them in the manner of philosophers, and if you will even by fertilizing them with the Cartesian spirit, or rather by systematizing the ideas of Descartes in the manner of Kabbalists? Our pretensions do not exceed these limits, which we dare to believe quite reasonable; and in this case, whatever disdain Spinoza had for Kabbalah, it would only concerns the consequences (and they are very numerous) rejected by Spinoza, and this heavy paraphernalia, this imposing apparatus, this great methodical and instrumental side of the Kabbalist system that Spinoza could neither respect nor adopt without returning to his former masters, and without admitting all the errors that had forever alienated the Morteira and the Abuabs, finally all the Hebrew orthodoxy; this disdain, once again, could not have gone beyond these limits. And who is the one who warns us? It is Mr. Saisset himself in his learned introduction, where he does not fail to argue that Spinoza's ideas, in a very important point of his doctrine, offer very striking analogies with the Alexandrian doctrine. Why not say Kabbalistic doctrine instead? But, whether Mr. Saisset says so or not, he does not need anyone to remind him that one cannot have disdain for the Kabbalah and not have it for the Alexandrian doctrines. For it is not from today that these two doctrines, the Kabbalah and the Alexandrian school, have been judged, and rightly so, two systems that are not very dissimilar.

But this disdain, we repeat, has not yet been noticed, and we continue on our way. If it existed, we would find it difficult to understand, firstly, the two passages where, in our opinion, there is mention, and very honorable and respectful mention, of Kabbalistic doctrines, and secondly the analogies and unintentional similarities that Spinoza's ideas present with Kabbalistic ideas. I have said two passages and I insist on them, although Mr. Saisset has only spoken of one, which he tries to explain in the most appropriate way not to offend his favorite system; and I believe that the second passage, which Mr. Saisset seems to have completely neglected, has nothing to envy to the importance and interest of the first. If I have had any reward for my assiduous research on Spinoza, it is to have been able to glean after Mr. Saisset such a remarkable document for the history of the filiation of philosophical systems. It is only the first that is cited by Mr. Saisset. Let's stop at it for a moment and measure its extent, which Mr. Saisset seems to want to singularly shrink.

In the second part of the *Ethics*, in the scholia of Proposition VII, after repeating his mother idea that thinking substance and extended substance are one and the same substance, that in the same way a mode of extension and the idea of this mode are one and the same thing expressed in two ways, Spinoza adds:

This is what seems to have been seen as through a cloud by some Hebrews who maintain that God, the intelligence of God and the things it conceives, are one.[5]

Mr. Saisset seems to have no doubt that allusion is made here to Kabbalistic doctrines. We agree with him; only a few doubts were allowed, and he could have skillfully solved and clarified them. Wouldn't Spinoza have thought of some other system of philosophy among the Jews in writing these lines? Do these doctrines and expressions belong only to Kabbalists? One could really doubt it, since we know that Jewish philosophers outside of our Theosophists used the same phrases, perhaps even more similar, at least grammatically, to those of Spinoza. Why say the Kabbalists rather than the philosophers who, no less than these, have recognized and proclaimed the unity of the knower, of knowledge and the known thing, *Daat, Yodeah, Veyaduah*,[6] or of the intelligent, of intelligence and the extended thing, *Sekhel Maskil uMuskal*?[7]

Mr. Saisset decides the question in favor of the Kabbalists, and we have said that he is right. Here's why. In the first place, Spinoza did not keep silent the names of Iben Ezra, Maimonides, Gersonides, whenever the opportunity arose to name them. Why would he have hidden them this time under the vague and obscure phrase of *some Hebrews*? He does not blush, as we have seen, to borrow from a less illustrious Jewish writer, R. Hasdai Crescas, the true intelligence of Aristotle's words. How would he have removed unquestionably more famous names? These *some Hebrews* seem to be other people less known to the reader, but to whom Spinoza felt a lot of duty in his heart.

And then how did they say these things, according to Spinoza? How did these *some Hebrews* glimpse at this precious unity? He's going to tell us: *like through a cloud*. However, we believe that as much as this expression vividly paints us the method and the obscure, metaphorical style of the Kabbalists, it is repugnant and seems inappropriate when it comes to philosophers such as our peripatetic rabbis who have always expressed themselves in philosophy in a clear, natural and intelligible way.

Finally, let us probe, if possible, the relative meaning of the sentences that the Dutch philosopher would have had in mind, and by comparing them with his own system and his own ideas, let us see where they appear more similar to us, and, therefore, which, among all these sentences, he may have thought of preferentially. What is the Spinozist doctrine that we want to see in the ideas of *some Hebrews* ? It is that from the single Substance flow the Thinking Substance and the Extended Substance, which form with it only one and the same Substance. Here we have three terms of comparison with the *Yodeah, Daat, Yaduah,* or *Sekhel, Maskil uMuskal* of the philosophers, and the *Sepher, Sopher, Sippur*[8] of the Kabbalists. Which of these three triads meets the three terms of Spinoza? If there was only the middle term, that is to say the thinking substance, we would not dare to decide the question, and the doubt, in our opinion, would be very difficult to dispell; but we have the first term and the last, the single substance and the extended substance, and we do not hesitate to declare that it is a thousand times more to the corresponding terms of the Kabbalistic triad that these two terms answer than to their equivalents that we have just seen in our philosophers. The idea of the single substance, which is the first of these two terms, responds a hundred times better to the crown (*Keter*[9]) of the Kabbalistic triad, that is to say to the *Sepher* or Book, which expresses, with the consent of all the connoisseurs of Kabbalah, the idea of supreme substance, and it is only because this meaning seems to us beyond doubt that we will give the reader the proofs that could demonstrate it.[v] Now, is it the same with *Yodeah*, or the *Sekhel* of philosophers? Never, as far as I know, did the idea of substance enter into the intention of these authors, and never has anyone claimed to interpret their formula in this way. The ontological meaning has remained constantly foreign to these philosophical formulas, which propose only the simple analysis and the economy of divine intelligence, apart from any ontological consideration in relation to other existences; and there are not even the very names that Kabbalists and philosophers have used to express their ideas that do not reveal to us the profound difference that separates them, the Kabbalistic *Sepher* being as apt to express the idea of substance as *Yodeah* and *Maskil* are incapable of.

It is therefore the kabbalistic *Sepher* that Spinoza claimed to identify with the supreme substance indicated.

---

v. Mr. Franck does not understand the Crown in any other way. But what is the Crown in the allegorical language of Kabbalah? It's the Substance. (*Kabbalah*, part. II, p. 199.)

It is from it that thinking substance and extended substance branch, which are one and the same substance with the former. As for the thinking substance, we said that there would be no sufficient reason to see it rather in the Kabbalistic *Sopher* than in the *Daat* or *Maskil* of the philosophers. But, as for the extended substance, it is quite another thing; and we dare here again to affirm that nothing is more suitable to give rise to the idea of extension than the *Binah*[10] or the Kabbalistic *Sippur*, as nothing is further from this idea than the *Muskal* or the *Yaduah* (the known thing or rather the concept) of the philosophers. We do not need long philosophical developments to prove this; the mere mathematical or alphabetic symbology attached to these two terms is sufficient to demonstrate it: for, if the *Hokhma*[11] or wisdom is represented by the Point or the *Yod*[12], the *Binah* (*Sippur*) is expressed by the *He*[13] or all the three dimensions, that is to say all the elements of extension.

Here, we almost touch the point of divergence where Spinoza, by detaching himself from the esoteric doctrine of *some Hebrews*, embarks on an adventure according to his individual reason; and by taking a wrong step, by confusing two things that this doctrine had always distinguished, he slipped, and with him his system, into a genuine pantheism, attesting by his very fall that the difference between Spinoza and Kabbalah is the very difference between Kabbalah and pantheism, a difference that appears here in all its light. For, if the Kabbalists gave to the *Binah*, to the *Sippur* (Kabbalistic narrative) the characters of extension, it is not in the proper and natural sense, as we well know, but only in the purely metaphorical sense, in order to express the intellectual object, the logical thing[vi], in a word, the ideal matter, by the same qualities that constitute bodily matter, the true extension. To express the latter, to designate true matter, it is not in the *Binah*, in the Mother Superior, as our Theosophists say, that it must be sought; rather it is in the inferior Mother, in the kingdom (*Malkhut*[14]), crown too — *Ateret*[15], in the Daughter always resembling the mother and her

---

vi. Basically, the *Sepher*, *Sopher* and *Sippur* of the Kabbalists, are nothing other than this: the subject, the object and the act of thought; unless one understands them not only in a logical sense, but also in an ontological sense. With this reservation made, we are happy to agree with Mr. Franck in *Kabbalah* (part. II, p. 145), although for him this meaning does not seem sufficiently demonstrated.

As for us, we believe that he guessed right, and could he doubt it after establishing on page 188 that wisdom and intelligence are only the subject and the object? However, if there is something indubitable, it is that the Crown, Wisdom and Intelligence, are precisely the same as the *Sepher*, *Sopher*, *Sippur*, and therefore the same interpretation suits both. R. M. Cordovero, quoted by Mr. Franck himself, would be enough of an unquestionable authority, and, what is more, he offers us Kabbalistic thought in the same form that Spinoza attributes to *some Hebrews*, so it would be a safe bet that it was perhaps this same passage of Cordovero that Spinoza had in mind.

Let us hear it from him: "The first three *Sephiroth*, namely, the Crown, Wisdom and Intelligence, must be considered as one and the same thing. The first represents knowledge or science; the second, what knows; and the third, what is known. To explain this identity, it is necessary to know that the science of the Creator is not like that of creatures: for in them science is distinct from the subject of science and relates to objects which, in turn, are distinct from the subject. This is what we mean by these three terms: thought, what thinks and what is thought. On the contrary, the Creator is himself both knowledge, what knows and what is known etc."(Cordovero in *Kabbalah*, part. II, p. 195.)

faithful Portrait; [vii] and precisely the extent or the extended substance of Spinoza, who, by coupling it to the thinking substance, *Hokhma*, and then identifying it with the supreme substance or *Keter*, clearly confused the Kabbalistic kingdom with intelligence, the daughter with the mother, bodily matter and ideal matter, and created in one fell swoop the principle and root of his pantheism. [viii]

We submit these assessments to the competent judges; as for us, we wanted from that moment to establish this important point of our examination, so that, going down to a more analytical study of the kabbalistic traces in Spinoza, we might hold in our hands like a thread leading us into this labyrinth.

The passage in question, where Spinoza admits that his doctrine was, although through clouds, anticipated by *some Hebrews*, is the first of those that attest in favor of Spinoza's borrowings from the Kabbalistic system, and it is the one that is quoted and to a certain extent, appreciated by Mr. Saisset. The other no less interesting passage, which Mr. Saisset makes no mention of, is the one we read in his letters. He replied to Oldenburg, who had categorically invited him to explain the confusion between God and Nature that seemed to result from his system, a vital point if ever

---

vii. When Paul calls Jesus the figure of the Father's substance, he is only transporting from the great incarnation, the kingdom of the Kabbalists, a sacramental expression to put on the individual incarnation of the son of Mary. (See Bergier, *Dictionnaire*, vol. IV, p. 60.)

viii. In the sense that we give to *the* Malkhut (Kingdom), we differ, to our great regret, from the learned author of *Kabbalah*, who, on page 197, believes that he must understand it in a different way.

there was one, especially in Spinoza's philosophy, and especially still with regard to Kabbalah. What does the Jewish philosopher answer?

> But to tell you all my thoughts [he will therefore open his heart to us] on the three points you have marked, I will not hide, as far as the first is concerned, that I have in my soul an idea of God and Nature very different from that which the new Christians are accustomed to defend. [So he believed he agreed with the ancient Christians, probably because they, in turn, agreed with the ancient Jews.] I believe that God is the immanent cause of all things, as they say, and not the transitory cause. I declare it with Paul: "We are in God, and we move in God." I must also say that this was the sentiment of all the ancient Hebrews, [ix] as can be conjectured from certain traditions, however disfigured they may be in a thousand ways. [x16]

Here no doubt is possible. If the first passage examined leaves our judgment somewhat floating between the two conclusions, if it takes some argument to succeed in seeing in it a reference to Kabbalah, here it is Spinoza who walks to his goal with an assured step; if there it was necessary to lift a corner of the

———————————

ix. What a difference between Spinoza's sentence and the ironic expression of R. Saadia, who, speaking of the belief in metempsychosis, says that it is professed by people who call themselves *Yehudim* (Jews)! Kabbalists might say that no one is better suited to this title than they are, if it is true, as we read in the *Talmud*, that anyone who is not an idolater is called *Yehudi* (*Talmud Meghila* [כל הכופר בעבודה זרה נקרא יהודי, מגילה יג ע"א]). We are very close to Salvador when, declining his first and last names at the Tribunal of Humanity, he declares his name to be Praiser (translation of *Yehudi*). (See *Rome, Paris and Jerusalem*.)

x. *Works of Spinoza*, Volume II, p. 339.

veil to discover Kabbalistic allusions, here they show themselves in their nakedness. The reader has already sensed a good number of them; let's try to write them down, too. The idea in itself could not be more suitable for the system of Kabbalah; and whatever opinion one has of the reproach of pantheism directed against this system, one cannot disagree that the idea of the immanent cause, if it exists somewhere in Hebraism in a somewhat philosophical way, it is undoubtedly in this system. And what does Spinoza want to conclude by this? It is that God and Nature are not terms as disparate as may be believed; that their separation is entirely modern; and although the Kabbalists did not absolutely identify, in the manner of Spinoza, God with Nature, yet their union is at least infinitely closer in their system than in any other within Hebraism, so close that it has not been spared the accusation of pantheism. What else could we want to see in the passage in question but an allusion to Kabbalah?

But it's not just the idea itself that makes the case for our interpretation. Spinoza expresses himself in such a way that it would take deep-rooted prejudices not to see that he is talking, to anyone who wants to hear, about the mysterious tradition of the Jews. One word, however, about the phrase we are reading here: the sentiment of *all the ancient Hebrews*. — It is quite otherwise that he points out this class of Jews in his first passage; it is, we remember, by the much humbler designation of *some Hebrews*. We will ask: how could it be the same people, the same system, under two denominations so different? But, if we think about the words of our author, the objection will vanish by itself.

Which Hebrews are these? The *ancient* Hebrews; it was they who had a unanimous sentiment on this, it was they who recognized without controversy a truth that was revoked in doubt by the moderns; and this is, shall we say, the language that would invariably be used by anyone who would admit, as Spinoza seems to admit, the antiquity and legitimacy of the Kabbalistic system. This is why he speaks here of *all the ancient Hebrews*, precisely because they are the elders, while in the other passage they are only *some Hebrews*, because he refers to the present time, when unanimity had ceased to reign in this.

But what is the past to which the Amsterdam philosopher turns? Is it the closest past, the rabbinical past, the one that preceded him by a few centuries? No, it is not that recent past whose authority Spinoza invokes. It is, above all, the midrashic talmudic past, it is, even further, the prophetic and biblical past, and the latter past no less obviously than the other, the rabbinical past. For, let it not be forgotten, this immanent cause which Spinoza credits here to the honor of the Hebrew past, which he considers on his metaphysical side, he has already once before attributed to Scripture, to the Prophets; not, indeed, in its philosophical form, but in a very critical sense, that is to say all the times, and they are very numerous, that it happens to him in his theological-political treatise to explain the style, the biblical phraseology, and this constant intervention of the Godhead in all the moral, intellectual and physical phenomena of nature.

Is it only the biblical past that Spinoza has before his eyes, and is it ultimately only a simple allusion to biblical Hebraism, without any possible application to

Kabbalistic doctrines? Beware of believing it. Spinoza himself takes care of enlightening us on this. For, see, this same doctrine of the immanent cause, this same union, not to say unity, of God and Nature, which he attributes here to all the ancient Hebrews, it is, in its constituent elements, the same theory that he says, in the other passage, to have been glimpsed through clouds by some Hebrews; proof, if there ever was, that, if he attributes it there to *some* and here to *all* Hebrews, it is only because of the difference in time he considers, the theory itself being quite identical under different names. It is about God Himself and Nature. As God is here declared one, if not one with Nature, the first substance is proclaimed there identical with the thinking substance and the extended substance, or, to speak in the language of *some Hebrews*, God, the intelligence of God, and the things understood by God, form one and the same thing. Do we want another solemn confirmation of the identity of the two theories? Let us see what Spinoza writes on page 339 and why he writes it. He addressed Oldenburg, which had complained to him, in the letter of November 15th, that, according to many, he confused God with Nature in the *Ethics*. Now, where does this confusion seem more flagrant than in the scholia of Proposition II (Part 2)[17], where the thinking substance, the extended substance, where the intelligence of God and the things it conceives, are declared to form only one substance with God? And it is here that Spinoza appeals to *some Hebrews*; precisely as in the letter to Oldenburg he mentions the disfigured traditions of the Hebrews about the same theory, the confusion of God with Nature. And if the theory is the same, how can we argue that he has only the language and phrases of the Bible in mind here?

And could the doubt still persist after what follows in the second passage? Spinoza does not appeal to the Bible, which would have opened its pages to anyone, which would have spoken, not by conjecture, but by common, popular phrases, of a well-known poetry; he does not appeal to the Bible, not because it is not comprehended in his thought but because, as it is a question of metaphysics, he must base his reasoning on a basis that does not float under him at the whim of the poetic breath, which does not lend itself to interpretations other than rigorously metaphysical, because it is Spinoza himself who warns us, in the *Theological-Political Treatise*, that it is in vain that we would seek throughout the Bible not only any philosophy, but any reasoning a little ordered and regular.

But he appeals to *"what can be conjectured of certain traditions, however disfigured they may be in a thousand ways"*. Every word has its value here. If he says he is conjecturing, he seems to point his finger at the Kabbalistic books, which, far from speaking to us in a clear, intelligible language, always hide their thoughts under enigmas that can only be understood by conjecture. If he does not simply say tradition, but certain traditions, he shows that it is a part, a particular class of Hebrew traditions, which are here in question, and at the same time he depicts with a single stroke the little knowledge that we generally have of them. But these traditions, Spinoza adds, are disfigured in a thousand ways. Where are these disfigured traditions that exist in Judaism? Is it the legal, ceremonial, ritual tradition of the Talmud? Far from it. First of all, the latter is not certain traditions, but *the* tradition, and far from being disfigured in a thousand ways, it is only too clear and precise by its detailed and numerous prescriptions. Above all, what possible relationship is there between this Talmudic tradition and the theory of the immanent cause? No, no! Everything tells us, in this text of Spinoza, that it is the esoteric tradition of the Jews that he invokes, and consequently also, as we saw earlier, that it is this same tradition that speaks in the *Ethics* through the organ of *some Hebrews*. Here ends everything we had to say about the clues that show us Spinoza initiated into the mysteries of the Jewish tradition, and drawing from them with full hands his most important theories. And here, therefore, ends the purely critical work that we proposed to ourselves. Later, when we shall say a word about the belief in metempsychosis, perhaps a phrase that escaped Spinoza will bring us back to the Kabbalists and their dogmas.[xi]

In the meantime, we are going to undertake a summary review, a rapid reexamination of Spinoza's main ideas. We shall not make a complete methodical analysis, the task would be beyond our strength; it is the impression left in us by the reading of certain passages of capital importance, it is the relationship and the striking resemblance with Jewish theology that we have seen, that we will expose as best we can. May competent judges go beyond our modest work

---

xi. Since this work cannot embrace all parts of Spinoza's philosophy, as we had flattered ourselves to do, we will immediately say where the allusion we believe we see lies. It is in *Ethics*, page 205, where, after speaking of the changes that the body itself undergoes, to the point of no longer being what it once was, of personal non-identity, he adds those words that, for lack of suitable developments, we ask readers to examine at their source.

and penetrate into the depths where our weakness and the insufficiency of our lights have prevented us from reaching.

We have, it seems to us, found in Spinoza a very clear, explicit, and, moreover, reiterated allusion to Kabbalistic beliefs. But what will not have escaped the attentive readers is that, by a luck that we would not have dared to hope for, this allusion, this revelation made by the author himself, it is on the occasion of the capital point of his doctrine[xii] that he made it, that is to say about the identity of the extended substance and the thinking substance with the indefinite supreme substance. The previous examination has already shown us many things: that this triad responds to the first triad of the Kabbalists, that the first substance responds to the Crown (*Keter*), that the thinking substance responds to Wisdom (*Hokhma*, the *Sophia* of the Gnostics), and that the extended substance responds to Intelligence (*Binah*); and just as, in Spinoza, Thought and Extension flow from Substance, just as both are basically one with the first, so also Wisdom and Intelligence eternally come out of the Crown, and constitute with it an indivisible unity expressed by the smallest of the letters, by the *Yod*, and by its three parts: the head, the body and the tail.

---

xii. This astonishing conformity in the supreme principles of two philosophies could not but be glimpsed by a prominent philosopher and writer to whom Kabbalah owes its first entrance into the world in the nineteenth century; we have named Mr. Franck, who, in his book *Kabbalah*, part. II, p. 193, after noting in Jewish theology the identity of thought and existence, adds that it allows us to glimpse what the meeting of Plato and Spinoza can achieve.

But let's take each of the three Spinozian substances separately, and compare it with its Kabbalistic equivalent. The supreme substance of Spinoza is also freedom and absolute activity. Is this a thought unknown to Kabbalists? Let's see. And first for the activity, the Crown is called *Mazal*[18], and the meaning of this name, it is the Kabbalists who give it to us. In the ordinary language of the Bible and the rabbis, it is the stars, it is also Fate, the *Fatum* that *Mazal* means; and the Kabbalists, by not disavowing this language and by applying in their metaphysical sense the ideas of Fate, of *Fatum*, to the Crown, offer us, on the one hand, the means of bringing them closer to the theogony of the Greeks, who placed the *Fatum* and Necessity at the top of their Olympus; and on the other, they also approach Spinoza singularly, who, in the number of characters that distinguish Substance, counts Necessity, just as the Kabbalists call *Mazal* the first of the *Sephiroth*[xiii]. It is not yet

---

xiii. They are also close to the Stoics to whom Josephus Flavius does not hesitate to assimilate the Pharisees, that is to say the Kabbalists under their old name; and above all, their *Mazal* could not be better compared than with the passages where Seneca justifies its application to Jupiter: *Vis illum Fatum vocare? Non-errabis. Hic est ex quo suspensa sunt omnia causa causarum* [*Naturales quaestiones*, lib. II, cap. xlv; "Would you call Him Fate? You wouldn't err. On him depends the cause of all causes"]. And there is not even the idea of suspension that does not bear a precious resemblance to the zoaristic formula: *haKol talui baMazal*, everything is suspended to the *Mazal* [הכל תלוי במזל זהר חלק ג קלד א]. This *Fatum* of Kabbalists and Stoics, which has nothing innumerable at bottom , can preside with impunity over the beliefs of a people of great passions and free activity. Is the same true of the *fatum* destructive of all freedoms? Benjamin Constant affirms it (*Du polytheisme romain*, tom. I, p. 18), however strange his assertion may seem. It is the opposite that I believe

the activity, we admit, but, if it is not in the *Mazal*, in this first meaning, there is to it another meaning completely arbitrary, quite conventional, quite special to the Kabbalists, and by the same token a hundred times more conclusive, which undoubtedly presents the idea of infinite activity, that is to say the idea of an eternal current that the Kabbalists discover in the name of the *Mazal*, and which they even express in another way by calling the first triad Eden, from which the river of Paradise eternally flows. But where in the Crown (*Keter*) is absolute freedom? Fortunately, here we do not have to lift any veil or to conjecture, because, something very rare, the Kabbalists speak to us without veil, without enigma. For them, the Crown is absolute Will, absolute Freedom, the *Ratson*[19], the Will of the Will (*Raava deRaavin*[20]), and if a digression did not take us too far, we would be keen to study what analogy there might be between Ibn Gabirol's philosophy, as Munk made it known to us, and this other singular philosophy that has occurred today on the other side of the Rhine, which places Will at the top of metaphysics, and Despotism at the top of politics, linking the one to the other and justifying the one by the other. This is not all: the three social states, liberty, filial dependence, we would be tempted to say filiality, and servitude, are distributed between

---

reasonable: it is in the fatalist a state analogous to that of the Buddhist, who aspires only to the annihilation of himself; for, just as the latter believes that thought has nothing better than to identify with universal thought, so the fatalist cannot believe that he has a serious will outside the universal will, which is unknown to him: it is rather towards apathy, inertia that he must lean rather than towards its opposite. Fatalism is therefore the nirvana of the will.

the three triads. It is true that these last denominations are attributed especially to the last member of each triad, and we will see of what immense consequence this crucial fact is in the examination that we will address of the confusion that Spinoza made between the third member of the third triad and the third of the first, between the ideal object and the material object, between the Mother and the Daughter, between *Binah* and *Malkhut*.

When, the first time, in bringing Spinoza's ideas closer to those of Kabbalah, I was struck by this conclusion, I thought I saw in it the key to Spinoza's pantheism and even the point that eternally separates Kabbalah from all pantheism. Whether I am wrong, the philosophical reader will say, but to me this confusion is obvious. What Spinoza says about extended substance, Kabbalists say about the last *Sephira*, the *Malkhut*, and if it were a book we wrote instead of an article, we would be more methodical, more abundant and more rigorous in the evidence; but within the very limits of an article, I dare say that we will not be less conclusive. By one of those rare phenomena that we saw about freedom and the divine will, here again the Kabbalists spoke without a veil. *Malkhut* is the extension, the place par excellence (*Makom, Atra*[21]); and every Israelite, even without thinking about Kabbalah, and by one of these ancient infiltrations into popular Judaism, says invoking God: Blessed be the *Makom,* blessed be He. But as Spinoza moved the *Malkhut,* the *Makom,* the extension, placing it in the personality of God, he said not only that the infinite extension is God himself, but also that God is an extended thing, *res extensa,* that bodies are in God (*of God,* prop. XV), because for him Extension is God; while the Kabbalists would have said that bodies are in extension, *Malkhut*, and that extension is in God. But it is not only as an extension that the third member of Spinoza's triad approaches the *Malkhut*, but also as Matter. Because, as we know, for Spinoza, the extended substance is matter, and all its developments would prove it if it were necessary. But, as we need means as decisive as they are summary, it is to his letter XXXVII that we refer the reader; for it is there that Spinoza identifies matter by an attribute that expresses an eternal and infinite essence.[22]

We would never end if we were to point out all the consequences of this first and capital confusion; let it suffices to note the one that was at all times the greatest reproach to Spinoza's moral system, that is to say, the negation of God's freedom. Whence this deplorable mistake? From having transported into God himself the extension, the matter, the domain of necessity, of true fatality;[xiv] from having put extension in the place of freedom, the *Malkhut* in the place of the *Dror*[23] (freedom); from having put the subjection, the servitude that is in the *Malkhut*, in the place of the freedom of the *Dror*, which is in the *Binah*; and if the name of freedom is preserved in God, it is only at the price of a profound alteration in its meaning, that one would find it very difficult to understand in Spinoza if the phraseology of the Kabbalists did not

---

xiv. This is how the Abbot Bergier rightly placed among those who deny the freedom of God, the philosophers who considered him as the soul of the world. (*Dictionnaire de Théologie*, p. XXXVII.) However, we know that the Kingdom is precisely the Soul of the World for Kabbalists. This is how Plato confused matter with necessity.

sometimes direct his pen. And here is, if I am not mistaken, a new abyss that the confusion of the two terms hollows out between Spinoza and Kabbalah, and which separates them in the moral order as it already separated them in the ontological order, as we have already observed above.[xv]

Thought and Extension remind us of the first two *Sephiroth* of the Pharisees, not only in themselves, but also by the place they occupy and the role they play in the system of Spinoza. What are Thought and Extension? They are the two attributes of God, the only ones we know of among his infinite attributes. Now, what is an attribute? "*I mean*", says Spinoza, "*by attribute what reason conceives in substance as constituting its essence.*" Here the attributes are far from what is usually understood by this word, pure

---

xv. It would be curious to discover how Spinoza, in our hypothesis, was able to deviate so much from the Kabbalistic doctrine that he fell into this confusion of ideal matter, of the ideal object with the material object. Perhaps Kabbalistic criticism was barely sketched, and such equivocation would not be impossible even today. Perhaps the countless nomenclature of the *Sephiroth* could have been a cause of error for Spinoza and made him believe, for example, that the name of *Rehovot* [רחובות], Extent or Extension, given to the *Binah*, allowed him to confuse it with Extension itself. In any case, the confusion of two emanations remains no less indisputable, as it is in my eyes no less likely in nascent Christianity, but in a sense quite opposite to that of Spinoza. With him, the ideal object is eclipsed by identifying itself with true extension. For Christianity, there is about the Holy Spirit a similar confusion between the Intellect and the Kingdom, both called by the Kabbalah by the name of Holy Spirit. But here the confusion is to the advantage of the first: of the ideal matter of the eternal object. The Kingdom is lost and vanishes within the Intelligence. Hence the contempt for matter and the world, and a thousand similar consequences.

qualities superimposed on the substance. They are the substance itself in its essentials, its elements or at most its natural radiations, inseparable from its being. Could a Kabbalist speak better about the *Sephiroth* or *Middot*[24] (attributes)[xvi], and especially about the first two, corresponding to the thought and extension of Spinoza, and which belong so intimately to the divine nature, and to what could Spinoza's definition be better suited than to these *Middot*, these *Sephiroth*? He is so close to the Kabbalists that (in the Schol. of prop. X, *of God*)[25] he seems to share their fears, their scruples, and he feels the need to justify his extraordinary definition against the reproach of multiplying substances that could be addressed to him. To hear him speak, one would think him a Kabbalist on guard against the danger of introducing multiplicity into God through attributes. And if he comes to the end of turning this pitfall, it is by pushing even to exaggeration the existence of these attributes in God, it is by admitting an infinite number of which thought and extension would be only imperceptible atoms, it is, in a word, by approaching this other side of the Kabbalistic doctrine because, it too, without going out of its decade, pushes to infinity the number of the attributes of God in a way that we do not want to judge here or even try to make intelligible, but only to expose, that is to say by positing that each *Sephira*, or member of the Decade, gives birth to another Decade; and each *Sephira* of this second Decade, to

––––––––––––––

xvi. In our opinion, this name of *Middot* does not have the meaning that Mr. Franck sees in it, and above all is not excluded from the second trinity, as he seems to believe. (*Kabbalah*, p. II, 198.)

another Decade, and so on to infinity.[xvii] And to speak more especially of Wisdom and Intelligence (the Thought and Extension of Spinoza), each of them consists of the ten *Sephiroth*, consequently of a second wisdom and a second intelligence, which, in their turn, give birth to a third, and thus to infinity. If this were the place to appreciate the value and the relative meaning of the two systems, we would take care to note, besides a striking resemblance, a no less remarkable difference that characterizes the two systems: because, while for Spinoza the unknown infinity has no analogy with this small part that we know, and therefore a somewhat complete knowledge is forbidden to us, for Kabbalists, on the contrary, it is only new aspects, infinite aspects that remain to be known, but always retaining a generic identity with the little that we know.

But if Thought and Extension, if the very role they play in Spinozism, if attributes such as Spinoza understands them, all bring us back to Kabbalistic theories, we now want to ask ourselves what meaning

---

xvii. In addition to the infinity of attributes that emerge from this singular theory and that brings us even closer to Spinoza, there is also a side where, far away from Spinoza's thought, Kabbalah seems to rub shoulders with the Christian theory of circumincession, surpassing it however by grandeur and fertility. It is quite the opposite for Spinoza, who admits between the attributes of God neither action nor possible relationship, and seems to want to separate them all the more in their course that he has united and confused them in their source. It would be worth reflecting on the causes and consequences of this remarkable difference. Meanwhile, the Christian circumincession reminds us of one of the oldest forms given to the *Sephiroth*, the shape of concentric circles.

Spinoza's Modes could have, and if it is possible to link them to these same theories. Substance, attributes and modes, these are the three categories, the three supreme *genera* in which Being appears to us. Does this division have a foundation in Kabbalah, and can we see its inspirations here again? If I am not mistaken, the three worlds of the Kabbalists respond to this triple division. *Beriah*, *Yetsirah* and *Assiah*[26] represent in them the substance, attributes and modes of Spinoza. It would be too long to set out here the reasons which, in our opinion, allow this identification; only we cannot help but observe here a curious distinction drawn by Spinoza himself, coming to the aid of our hypothesis. This is the distinction between *naturating nature* and *naturated nature*. Hence this distinction in Spinoza's system? We do not think we are risking too much by assuring that this is, to see, only a kabbalistic reminiscence and a happy inconsistency in the Spinoza system. But what is important for the distinction in question is to know where, according to Spinoza, naturating nature ends and where naturated nature begins. Is it attributes, is it modes? It seems that Spinoza has not explained this sufficiently, if we judge in the entirely hypothetical way in which Mr. Saisset expresses his opinion. It's modes, he says, and we believe he's right. Now, according to the Kabbalistic concordance, it is scarcely doubtful to which of the three worlds Spinoza's mode would respond. It is, as we can see, the *Assiah*, and it is precisely it wich brings together all the characters suitable for expressing the mode. Only a full discussion could give this point all the philosophical evidence.[xviii] But there are no less peremptory and much more abbreviated ways: it is to consult the rich nomenclature that belongs to the Kingdom, headquarters of *Assiah*. In this nomenclature, there are appellations that cast a beautiful light on the third category of Spinoza, and receive some in turn.

Thought and Extension belong, without a doubt, to the attributes of substance; but there is something else in Spinoza's system whose place does not seem beyond dispute. And first, what is Spinoza's *Idea of God* in the system of Kabbalah? I think I can say without rashness that it was the *Tiferet*[27], the *Logos*, that served as the basis for Spinoza's conception. However, if the opinion of Mr. Saisset, who places the Idea of God in naturated nature, were accurate, this kabbalistic correspondence would become impossible, and not only would all the indications that prove it, and that will be exposed soon, become inexplicable, but we would see reversed by this very fact the most likely harmonies. Is Mr. Saisset's opinion accurate? It is proposition XXXI of *De Deo* that has given rise, as it appears, to this assumption. It is here, indeed, that Spinoza says in express terms that the understanding, whether finite or infinite, must relate to naturated nature. And that explains what he means by understanding:

> By understanding, indeed, we obviously do not designate absolute thought, but only a certain mode of thinking, which mode differs from others, such as desire, love, etc.[28]

---

xviii. I have no doubt that any reader somewhat familiar with Kabbalistic doctrines will see, at a glance, the concordance of Spinoza's modes with Kabbalistic *Assiah*.

We could say first of all: Why, if it is the same thing, call it by two names that can awaken two different ideas? Why this departure from a uniformity of language which constitutes one of the most salient merits of this writer, and which is of extreme necessity in such obscure metaphysics? But, then, is it really the Idea of God that Spinoza so often speaks of in such magnificent terms? This mode, which differs from other modes, such as desire, etc., is it by chance that Idea of God referred to on page 52, P. II, Prop. IV: "*The Idea of God, from which derive an infinity of infinitely modified things, can only be unique*"?[29] Is this a language that suits a simple mode of naturated nature? However, it will be said, it is here that he refers to the proposition XXX, Part I, and seems to consider as the same thing the infinite understanding and the Idea of God.[30] But let us carefully weigh Spinoza's sentences, and we will see that the infinite Understanding of proposition XXX, that we quote here, is Intelligence insofar as it constitutes a part of Thought, that is to say, as he expresses himself in proposition XXXI, for example: will, desire, love, etc. How far from this fragmentary idea is the Idea of God! The Idea of God is, without a doubt, the thinking subject who takes full possession of the entire object; it is the entire infinite Thought, reflected entirely on itself. And the understanding of proposition XXXI, what is it? It is, Spinoza told us, "*a mode that differs from other modes of Thought*". It might be a lot but it's nothing in comparison. He will tell us, in proposition XXXII, that it is only the act of understanding, intellection, precisely as by will he means nothing other than the act of will, volitions, mocking all those who make of the will anything more than a vain abstraction.[31] In good faith, is this Spinoza's Idea of God?

Is this, let us say more, this other Understanding that Spinoza qualifies, in his letter XXXI[32], page 419, of the significant name of absolutely infinite, which he proposes to L. Meyer as an example of things immediately produced by God, and which contrasts so singularly with this other understanding of proposition XXXI, Part I, which is defined "*a certain mode of thinking and which differs from other modes*"? And if it is only that, if the Idea or the Intelligence of God is only this act of understanding, this intellection, what right do we have to proclaim that between the Intelligence of God and ours there is no greater resemblance "*than between the celestial sign Dog and the barking animal dog*"? What right does it have to raise this Intelligence so high, to tell us that it "*constitutes the essence of God*"? By no means! A "*mode that differs from other modes*", an intellection, would have deserved this honor?

We asked ourselves these questions when a doubt arose in our minds: if the Idea of God is not an attribute (besides Thought and Extension, Spinoza does not know a third), if it is not, all the more so, the supreme Substance; finally, if it is not even a mode, as we have just affirmed, then what is this Idea and what place should we assign to it? That is an objection, and I believe it to be the most serious.

But first, we could observe not without plausibility that the Idea of God, according to Spinoza, is, all things considered, Thought itself in its relations with Extension, the subject in its relations with the object, precisely in the same way as for Spinoza the Man is only the Idea of the body united to the body;

rapprochement all the more precious that the Idea of God or the Logos, is for the Kabbalists the supernal Man, the Man par excellence, the active and passive Man at the same time. Is that all? and won't we have a better answer? No, no doubt, provided we think about it for a moment. And in fact, where is the strength of this objection, where is the basis on which it is based? It is based, as everyone can see, on the assumption that between the attribute and the mode, the mode as we understand it, as Spinoza himself understands it, neither eternal nor infinite, and which constitutes naturated nature, there is no middle, and that Spinoza's system leaves no room for anything that is neither. Now, let us hasten to say, this assumption is nothing less than proven, and we would not have dared to admit this lack of coherence, this lack of rigor in a system so well connected, so compact, so homogeneous, so geometric, if an authority that we like to revere had not driven all scruples from our minds, and had not itself given Spinoza's Idea of God an honorable place in this system, where, without sitting among the attributes, it does not stoop to the modes, as we understand them and as Spinoza himself understands them in general. And to whom do we owe this unexpected help? We owe it to Mr. Saisset. It is in his admirable *Introduction* that he makes this important remark. We cannot express it more forcefully than he does himself:

> It is generally believed that in Spinoza's doctrine, between God taken in himself and the finite and mobile beings that make up the universe, there are no intermediaries other than the infinite attributes from which modes emanate, and which themselves emanate from Substance.

This prejudice is a serious mistake, and I dare say that whoever has it in mind has only a very incomplete idea of Spinoza's speculations.[33]

And these intermediaries, seen by Mr. Saisset, what are they? They are

modes of a very different nature, modes proper, eternal, infinite, more closely related than souls and bodies to Substance.[34]

At least, in these eternal and infinite modes there will be no more to distinguish. By no means! For Spinoza, it is also Mr. Saisset who announces to us, there are

two kinds of eternal and infinite modes [we are not yet to the true modes, the modes proper], those which derive from the absolute nature of an attribute of God and those which derive from them and which are hence separated from Substance by two intermediaries.[35]

And the Idea of God, to what modes will it belong? To the first kind, says Mr. Saisset, that is to say, to the eternal and infinite modes, which immediately flow from Substance.

Would he, Spinoza, for these eternal and infinite modes, have expressly declared that they belong to naturated Nature? Would he, as Mr. Saisset (*Introduction*) assures, have highly proclaimed that the Idea of God is the first degree of naturated Nature in the order of thought?

It is to *De Deo*'s twenty-first proposition that Mr. Saisset refers us; but it is in vain that we would seek the qualification of Mode attributed to the Idea of God, and all that is read is *"that it derives from the absolute nature of an attribute of God"*.[36] This language might still not be clear enough and still leave room for doubt that the Idea of God must belong to naturated Nature. But we shouldn't rush to that conclusion. We have a curious correspondence between Meyer and Spinoza, which provides us with valuable information on this.

If I understood their feelings correctly, Meyer is obsessed with the same prejudice that Mr. Saisset authorizes today by his science and his name; and Spinoza himself comes to overthrow with his own hand the prejudice, this inaccurate interpretation of his words. Could anything be more convincing? Instead, let's rather listen to his friends. It is Meyer who, in the letter XXX, asks Spinoza for an example of the things immediately produced by God and those produced by some modification, and, like Mr. Saisset, he immediately adds conjecturally:

> Thought and Extension, it seems to me, belong to the first category; understanding in Thought, movement in Extension, to the second.[37]

Spinoza answers; he corrects, rectifies, overturns his friend's hypothesis; finally he interprets it himself, as we interpret it today. Meyer had put in his first category only the attributes; Spinoza answers:

> For the first category, I will mention in Thought the absolutely infinite Understanding.[38]

It was precisely this Understanding that Meyer proposed to him to place among the infinite modes. Spinoza, on the contrary, places it suddenly in the first category, characterizing it however as absolutely infinite, so that it is not confused with that other understanding which, although infinite, regards, as he himself says, only one of the faculties, for example desire, love, etc., and contrasts so obviously, by the same token, with the absolutely infinite Understanding, which is the same thing as the Idea of God, that is to say, as Spinoza defines it, the Idea of all the attributes of God...

Arrived at this point, we cannot question the words and not insist on the more or less accuracy that there would be to call the Idea of God, in the language of Spinoza, a mode. Whether or not it is a mode, it remains demonstrated that nothing prevents us from seeing the Logos, Beauty, the *Tiferet* of the Kabbalists, the first emanation after Thought and Extension, the first product of the attributes of God.

But we have much more direct and positive reasons that persuade us. And first, let's see if the generation of the Word, of the Logos of the Kabbalists, is the same as the origin and derivation of the Idea of God. For Kabbalists, the Logos, *Daat* as they call it, is the result of the union of Wisdom and Intelligence, Thought and Spinoza's Extension. This is their son, the first born. It is the subject, Wisdom, who by taking possession of his object gives birth to a son in his likeness. As we can see, for the Kabbalists it is not the first substance, the Crown to which Wisdom (*Hokhma*) turns; it is Intelligence, it is she who is the object with whom she is united; it is by uniting with her that Wisdom brings the Son in her image out of her womb. Is it to Extension (responding to the *Binah*, Intelligence of the Kabbalists) that Thought unites in the Spinoza system? Is it Extension, the object of his Intelligence? Mr. Saisset denies it; and by denying it, by admitting on the contrary that it is the absolutely indeterminate Being, the first Substance, which is the object of the divine Thought, he cannot hide from himself *"that it is one of the most obscure points of Spinoza's metaphysics"*;[39] and he is surprised (and how could he not be surprised?) that one can separate the Thought of the Substance from the Thought of its attributes. As for us, no offense to Mr. Saisset, we conceive the Idea of Spinoza much differently. We believe that the object of Thought is not Substance, as Mr. Saisset assumes, but Extension, or, if we still wish, the other attributes of God; in a word, that Spinoza's Thought is the Thought not only of Substance, but also of its attributes. If we did not have other evidence, there would already be a good chance that it was so by what we know from Spinoza about the elements that make up our being. No one who has even glimpsed the narrow chain that links all the parts of his metaphysics will dare to deny, I believe, that the Idea of the body and the body of which man is made, according to Spinoza, are only an image, only a reproduction in a lower sphere of Thought and Extension. For him, the same relationships, the same laws that govern Thought and Extension, also govern the soul and the body. Thus, as the two attributes of Substance follow in their developments two parallel lines without action and without reciprocal influence, so the soul is powerless to communicate motion to matter, and the latter could never contribute to the formation of

Thought. Now, what is the object of the soul or the Idea of the body according to Spinoza? It is the Body and nothing but the Body, it is at the same time its object and its limit. He teaches it unequivocally and unambiguously:

> The object of the Idea which constitutes the human soul, is the body, in other words a certain mode of Extension [xix].

And the mode of Extension (the Body) is so well the object and the only object of this mode of Thought (the soul), that Spinoza is not afraid to assert that as a Body is more apt than others to act or to suffer simultaneously from a greater number of forms, it is united to a soul more apt to perceive simultaneously a greater number of things. [xx] And we could without rashness assert of the Model, that is to say of the Thought and the Extension in God, what Spinoza so peremptorily affirms of its Copy and its reflection, and also say in our turn, without fear of a denial from Spinoza, that just as the object of the mode of Thought (the soul) is only the mode of Extension, the Body, so also the object of Thought, it is Extension itself, or, to speak in the language of the Kabbalists, that the object of the Wisdom, is not the Crown (the First Substance), but rather the Intelligence, the Extension of Spinoza, and finally that the Idea of God of Spinoza is only the result of this union, like the Logos, the Beauty of the Kabbalists.

---

xix. *De Anima*, Proposition XIII. [*Objectum ideæ humanam mentem constituentis est corpus sive certus extensionis modus actu existens et nihil aliud.*]

xx. *Ibid.*, Schol.

But, to know Spinoza's opinion on the subject of Thought, we are not, thank God, doomed to laboriously extract it from more or less likely comparisons or analogies. Mr. Saisset, who saw everything so well in Spinoza, how did he not realize that there is a passage in the *Ethics* whose interpretation cannot be doubted? And this is the one where Spinoza, we remember, seems to allude to his masters, the Kabbalists, however interposing clouds between their formulas and his own ideas, and saying that they only glimpsed his favorite Principle, generator of his entire system, through clouds. But what do they see beyond the clouds? It is that God, the Intelligence of God, and the things it conceives, are but one thing. Let's translate this language into Spinoza's, or rather let Spinoza interpret it himself, and what will we get? He himself tells us in formal terms: it is that thinking Substance and extended Substance are one and the same Substance, which is known sometimes by one of its attributes, sometimes by the other. As we can see, Spinoza identifies his doctrine with that of his *some Hebrews*, for whom things, the object that Intelligence conceives, is not the first, but the third term, that is to say the extended Substance of Spinoza. Imagine that for Spinoza the thing that Thought conceives is not Extension, but God himself, the First Substance, as Mr. Saisset claims: where would be then the much vaunted resemblance between Spinoza and the Hebrews whose authority he invokes? In our eyes, this is an argument so serious, so conclusive, that, if there is anything that prevents us from relying absolutely on it, it is only to see it so neglected by the great interpreter of Spinoza, Mr. Saisset, and it only needs his adhesion to print the seal of complete certainty. And as if Spinoza had wanted to unite the two reflections we have just made in the same bundle, he immediately adds:

> In the same way, a mode of Extension and the Idea of this mode are one and the same thing expressed in two ways.[40]

If there is therefore something probable in Spinoza's interpretation, it is that, in his opinion, Thought has as its object Extension, and we would not be afraid to add that the Idea of God is not the very act of thinking about Extension, as Mr. Saisset says, which belongs rather to Thought itself or to the Wisdom of the Kabbalists, but the result of their union, the product of the coupling of the subject and the object, the judgment, as the Kabbalists call the Logos itself (*Mishpat*), the Idea par excellence, the Law (*Torah*)[41], the Word, the Discourse. Are we reduced to this data on the generation of the Idea by Thought and Extension? No, says Spinoza, because the Idea of God is the Idea of his attributes of Thought and Extension (see part I, prop. xxx).

Let us translate Spinoza's Proposition into Kabbalistic language, and we will repeat with Mr. Franck:

> From their mysterious union [of Wisdom and Intelligence] comes a son [Spinoza will call him by this name later] who, according to the original expression, taking the features of both his father and his mother, bears witness to them both.[xxi]

---

xxi. *Kabbalah*, 189.

This Idea of God that nothing so far prevents us from identifying with Beauty, the Idea (*Daat*) of the Kabbalists, which by its very singularity should have made us suspect its foreign origin, and we will add by its isolation; which only makes short appearances in the system, to be erased soon, as Mr. Saisset himself noted; which is so obviously marked by the seal of the East and mystical ideas in general; which no less than the Idea of Extension, of which we will soon have to speak, presents striking analogies with Alexandrinism, as Mr. Saisset also admits in his *Introduction*, and one could a hundred times better say with Kabbalah; this Idea of God finally is declared by Spinoza, as we have seen, infinite and eternal as the Thought from which it derives. Is this an idle and inconsequential question? Yes, if we consider it in relation to Spinozism itself, and the abandonment where his author leaves it would prove it if necessary; no, if we link it to Kabbalistic ideas, or, to put it better, if we understand it in the sense of Kabbalists; if we conflate it, as we propose to do, with the Son, the Logos, the Word, the *Tiferet* of Kabbalists. The proof is that it occupies a considerable place in Kabbalistic speculations, and, by offering us a new link between Spinoza and his predecessors, it gives us a happy explanation, we dare to say the key to this pure, intelligible side of Spinozism.

Was it not among the Kabbalists that this question originated? Isn't it in them that it is really indigenous? Was it not in their schools that one first disputed whether the generation of the Logos, the Word, the *Tiferet*, was in *eternity* or in *time*? Was it not from their schools that the ancient Christians learned to question, and even to divide themselves in the solution of this problem? Is it not the same problem that, when resolved negatively, gave birth to Arianism, for which the Son, being an emanation of the Father, could not be of the same divine and eternal nature as the latter? Is it not in the Kabbalist system that it is really a part adhering to the whole, a branch united to the tree in a common sap and a common life, and not the host of a day, a moment, as in the philosophy of Spinoza? And yet how eloquent is this short appearance! What uniformity of ideas and language! what a deep and characteristic resemblance! The Logos, for the Kabbalists, is the place, the seat of all ideas, the center where everything ends, where everything connects and unites, the common link of all the *Sephiroth*: it is the tree of life that is in the middle of the Garden of Eden, and its central position is the sign, the symbol of its synthetic and unifying role expressed in the Kabbalistic nomenclature by *Ehad*[42], the unique par excellence. Now, what does Spinoza teach us about the Idea of God? That from it an infinity of infinitely modified things derive and that it can only be UNIQUE, as the Logos of the Kabbalists is the only one, as that of the Christians is the *unigenitus*.

But Spinoza himself will leave for a moment his natural, geometric language that could mask his borrowings, and speak the symbolic and metaphorical language of the secret theology of the Jews. It is true that we owe this unusual style to the Christianity professed by his friends, but finally Spinoza spoke and he himself applied to the Idea of God his corresponding name in Christian dogmatics, itself derived from that of the Jews. Let us appreciate, pray, as appropriate, the sentences that will follow; let us remember that our souls, the Ideas of Bodies, have their root, the perpetual source of their lives in the Idea of God, which contains all Ideas, all souls, and especially human souls, let it illuminate with its light as the Christian Word illuminates all men who come into this world, and as the Jewish Word, *Tiferet*, is itself the law, the rule, the light of spirits (*Torah — Or*); and after having seriously meditated on these precious indications, let us listen to Spinoza addressing Henri Oldenburg, who urged him to explain himself with regards to Jesus:

> Finally, to show you openly my thought on the third point, I say that it is not absolutely necessary for salvation to know Christ according to the flesh, but it is quite different if we speak of this SON OF GOD, that is to say of this eternal Wisdom of God which has manifested itself in everything and mainly in the human soul. It is it only that teaches us what is true and false, good and evil.

What is this Son of God of Spinoza? Is it simply human reason as it contemplates truth, philosophy? But it would have been a ridiculous bamboozlement by which Oldenburg would never have been fooled, and instead of insisting in his answer on the Incarnation only, considering the existence of the Word to be admitted, he would have urged his opponent to specify his language. No, I say it in all conviction, Spinoza believed in the Word, the uncreated, spiritual Jewish Word, and rejected only the Christian Word, that is to say the Incarnate Word.

> As for what some churches add, that God has assumed human nature, I have expressly warned that I do not know

what they mean; and, to speak frankly, I will confess that they seem to me to speak a language as absurd as that which would say that a circle has assumed the nature of a square. [xxii] [43]

Spinoza, in the question of the Word, was Jewish, entirely Jewish, and nothing but Jewish. [xxiii]

Spinoza spoke only the name of wisdom: the Idea of God could be here far from his thought. Make no mistake. Spinoza will clarify himself. He speaks in the fourth part of the *Ethics*, page 223, of freedom, of the knowledge of good and evil, and he establishes that the free man, that is to say, according to his definition, governing himself by reason alone, has no idea of evil or good; and he adds:

---

xxii. Letter VIII, page 339.

xxiii. We have sometimes wondered if Spinoza, with his kabbalistic sympathies on the one hand, his antipathies against the Christian Trinity and Incarnation on the other, did not represent the true Jew of the time of Jesus. And although it is affected today to believe among us that no possible analogy could exist between the teachings of Jesus and contemporary Jewish beliefs (see among others the beautiful work of Mr. Cohen, *Les Déicides*, p. 108), we doubt very much that we can ever demonstrate this state of mind. It would be easier for us to prove the contrary; but let us confine ourselves to saying, in the meantime, that without Kabbalah, that is to say, what is similar to Christianity, we could not explain the birth of this religion within Hebraism; and that without it too, that is to say, by what is in it dissimilar to Christian doctrines, we could not explain how all Jews did not become Christians. As for us, Spinoza is the true contemporary Jew of Jesus, and the scandal he took at the sight of certain Christian dogmas, the Incarnation especially, is the same scandal that Jesus' preaching produced among his ancestors.

And this is a truth that it seems that Moses wanted to represent, as well as some others already demonstrated in his History of the first man.

And later:

Later, this freedom was recovered by the Patriarchs guided by the Spirit of Christ, that is to say by the Idea of God.[44]

Valuable fragment of which we will try to list in a few words the most serious consequences.

1 — The story of the first man, that is to say the scene of paradise, the painting where, according to Spinoza, Moses wanted to represent the truth he claims to demonstrate, as well as some others already demonstrated. The scene of paradise, that is to say the theatre where, according to the Kabbalists, the external, historical representation of the most august truths of their theology develops in shortcut, where each source, each river, each name, each tree, each word has a very deep meaning, and it is precisely here, as we see, that Spinoza seeks a confirmation of his thoughts in the Mosaic words.

2 — And not only for the proposal in question, but also for a few others already demonstrated. These truths also have confirmation. Spinoza warns us about this in the History of Paradise. Now, what are these truths already demonstrated? No one knows; and nothing in Spinoza has come so far to make us suspect this resemblance that he displays here in broad daylight, and nothing has come so far to lift a corner of the veil that robs us of the source of his ideas. But he raises it himself, and he cries out to whoever wants to hear him that some other truths

already demonstrated by him, that is to say in the *Of God, Of the Soul*, etc., are represented by Moses in the account of paradise. A precious confession that must no longer leave any doubt in any loyal spirit about the kabbalistic derivation of Spinoza's ideas, even where he is silent, even where no allusion leads us back to it, since the present allusion is so general that it makes up for his past silence and satisfies all our requirements.

But let us not lose sight of the main object of these reflections; it is the Idea of God that we seek, it is the Word where we can see a reflection of the Kabbalistic verb. Now, as we have already seen, Spinoza leaves no room for any doubt about his intentions; the Spirit of Christ is the Idea of God, and it is by the Spirit of Christ or by the Idea of God that the Patriarchs have regained their freedom. There is no doubt that the Idea of God is for Spinoza as for the Kabbalists, Christ, the Logos, the Word, in a word the *Tiferet*, the son of wisdom and intelligence, of thought and extension. [xxiv]

---

xxiv. For Mr. Saisset, the object of Thought (the Wisdom of the Kabbalists) is not the attributes of God, but the absolutely indeterminate Being (the *Keter*, Crown); while these Attributes are indeed the object of the Idea of God (see his Introduction to *Ethics*). His sagacity and common sense immediately revolt against this hypothesis; and he is rightly surprised, "*because it does not seem that one can separate the thought of substance from the thought of its attributes*" (*ibid.*). He therefore proclaims this point, "*one of the most obscure points of Spinoza's Metaphysics*". Would he have bowed under the yoke of this hypothesis if he had taken more account of the Kabbalistic origin? It is permissible to doubt it: he would have seen that in them the object of thought (Wisdom) is not the Being, the indeterminate being (Crown), the *Non-ens*, but the *Binah*, the Extension of Spinoza.

But there are not here even secondary ideas that do not deserve serious attention. The Patriarchs? But why the Patriarchs alone? Why not also the prophets and the righteous who lived under the rule of the law? Why? But this is quite natural in Spinoza, since the Patriarchs, and the Patriarchs alone, are those who, according to the Kabbalists, have in some way repaired the sin of the first Adam: it was Abraham

---

Doesn't Spinoza himself reveal his thoughts enough to us? Far from it, in my opinion. It is he who, in order to express that the thinking Substance and the extended Substance are one and the same with the supreme Substance, appeals to the testimony of *some Hebrews* according to which God, the Intelligence of God and the things it conceives are one and the same. Now, the things that the intelligence conceives respond, as we see, to the extension of Spinoza, which is nevertheless the object of thought or what it conceives. He would prove it by what he says, that *"the object of the soul is the body; that the soul can only think of its body, which is both its object and its limitation. The object of the idea that constitutes the human soul is the body."* — (*De Anima*, pro. XXII.) Now it is known that Spinoza generally establishes the same relations between the soul and the body as between the thinking substance and the extended substance; for example, just as these two attributes follow, for him, two parallel lines without action and without crossing each other, so also, for him, the soul cannot determine the body to movements, nor can the body determine the soul to think. But if the object of Thought is not indeterminate Being but Extension and the other attributes, then what is the Idea of God? We answer that it is the Word. But what is the Word? It is not the act of thinking about the attributes of God, as Mr. Saisset asserts for Spinoza's Idea of God; but it is the eternal product of this act, the result of the union between the thinking subject and the thought object; it is the Logos, the discourse, the son resembling his father and his mother. This is the definition of the Word that Spinoza himself identifies, in his Letters, with his Idea of God. Let us listen to the Abbot Bergier, *Dictionnaire de Théologie*, vol. IV, p. 664.

who repaired his idolatry, Isaac who repaired his homicide, and Jacob finally who repaired his incest (*Zohar*, vol. III, p. III, 2).

The *Shekhinah*,[45] who had abandoned the earth after Adam and ascended to the seventh heaven, was recalled to the earth by the Patriarchs, guided, as Spinoza says, by the Spirit of Christ. — And in these last words, what teachings! For the God of the Pentateuch, the God who creates, who reveals himself, the creator and the revealer, is for the Kabbalists the Logos, the *Tiferet*; it is only to him that prophetic intelligence can rise; it is he who walks with Noah, with Abraham (*Genesis*), who walks in the cloud at the head of the Israelites; it is he, it is his spirit that constantly guides them, it is the Spirit of Christ, as Spinoza says to his Christian friend.[xxv]

And see the power of truth! Spinoza, in the series of emanations, has only set milestones. Logic will perfect his work. Between the *Tiferet*, the Idea of God,

---

xxv. This is the source of the strange doctrines of Saturninus and Basilides about the god of the Jews. They only pushed to absurdity and maliciously disfigured a belief that the Jews were the first to proclaim. They made the Logos, the Son, "*an angel of the last order, who, wishing to subdue the nations, had excited them against him, all princes, until the day when the supreme God sent* Noûs, *who was here below Jesus, son of Mary*". With these words, not only do these Gnostics abuse one of the Kabbalistic teachings, but they show us to which Jewish emanations responded, in their opinion, the Son of Mary, that is to say, the *Noûs*, who is in the Aeons of the Gnostics what the Wisdom of the Kabbalists is, and they thereby elevate Christ, who has his natural place in the Logos — or the *Yesod* (called by the Kabbalists Messiah), to this supreme emanation. Moreover, it is a very important research that would aim to establish in a plausible way which among all the Kabbalistic emanations has provided the most salient type and features of the Christian Word.

of Spinoza, and the Kingdom, the Idea of Extension, there is in the Kabbalistic series a middle term that responds, in the lower Triad, to the Thought, to the Wisdom of the upper Triad, and this is the *Yesod*, the foundation. We do not want to say anything about its meaning, preferring not to talk about it at all than to be condemned to express all our thoughts only briefly. But where is its equivalent in Spinoza? Nowhere, if we consult only him. For him, between the Idea of God and the Idea of Extension, no middle, no intermediary, no separation. Who will introduce it into Spinozism in the absence of Spinoza? Logic and Mr. Saisset. Let us see on page 89 of his *Introduction*,[46] where, as a result of such tight, convincing deductions, he forces us to admit between the Idea of God and the Idea of Extent another Idea of Thought about which Spinoza is silent, but which results rigorously from his premises and which fills the void left by the author in the series of the *Sephiroth*, by responding exactly to the *Yesod*, to the lower representation, to the image of thought, of the upper *Hokhma*, and also to the Idea of Thought or of the *Hokhma*, as the Idea of God is the Idea of the Crown or its representative, and as the Idea of Extension is the Idea of *Binah*, of intelligence, and its representative; finally a lower Triad responding to the upper Triad, just as in our mystics.

Do we need to add that the two systems could not be more similar than in the following. The most transparent analogy between Kabbalah and Spinoza is undoubtedly the Idea of Extension. The place it occupies in Spinoza is that which the Kingdom occupies in the Kabbalists; its relations with the attribute Extension of which it is the Idea, are the same relations which attach the kingdom to the intelligence, the daughter to the mother, the image to its model, the inferior mother to the superior mother; the proximate source, the immediate cause of the Idea of Extension and of the Kingdom is the same in the Kabbalists and in Spinoza. Among the first, it is Beauty, the Logos who gives birth to his future wife, just as the mother of all the living came out of Adam's rib. And in Spinoza, where does the Idea of Extension come from? Perhaps by consulting Spinoza it would be permissible to doubt it; but all doubt ceases as soon as Mr. Saisset is questioned. The truth speaks through his mouth in a way that is all the more eloquent because he was far from suspecting the consequences that we draw today in favor of our system, and that allows us to quote him a little against him:

> Now, from the Idea of God which immediately emanates from the divine Thought, Spinoza immediately emanates certain equally eternal and infinite modifications, and I believe I enter into his meaning by citing the IDEA OF EXTENSION as an example.[47]

We will spare the reader the scholarly argumentation that immediately follows. May his authority suffice for us. He returns to his beautiful discovery, on page 89, where he says again in express terms:

> The Idea of Extension is an emanation of the Idea of God, just as the Idea of God is an immediate emanation of the Thought of God.[48]

Two more characteristic marks, and we have finished identifying the Kingdom of the Kabbalists with the Idea of Extension. If there is something admitted, elementary among the Kabbalists, it is that the Kingdom is the seat of souls, the heavenly Jerusalem whose citizens are the dead or unborn souls. Now, who would believe it? this very idea is in Spinoza; it is in his Idea of Extension. Few words will suffice to demonstrate this, and here as elsewhere the learned interpreter of Spinoza will be our guide and our light:

> The Idea of Extension, comprises the ideas of all the modalities of Extension. But what is the idea of a modality of extension? It is a soul, a particular soul; the idea of Extension therefore envelops all souls; it is therefore literally the soul of the corporeal world. It is a universal soul, exactly like Plato and the Alexandrians, of which all particular souls are emanations. It is an infinite ocean of souls and ideas; every idea, every soul is a river of this ocean, every thought is a stream.[49]

May Mr. Saisset forgive us, but the omission of the name of the Kabbalists in this fragment seems incredible to us. Plato and the Alexandrians would have a kinship with Spinoza that would not have the Kabbalah which was so close to him; the disfigured traditions of which he claims to be the restorer would have none! Would they have nothing to do with this universal soul which is nevertheless one of the most important Kabbalistic conceptions, and which has little to envy either the soul of Plato or that of the Alexandrians? In truth, I can't believe it!

The second distinctive mark, we have just mentioned. The first is the seat of souls; the second, very similar to this one and its generalization, is the soul of the world. The Kingdom, like the Idea of Extension, is the soul of the world, the universal soul; it is the *Psyche* of Plato and the Neo-Platonists, whose name it bears translated into Hebrew by *Nefesh*,[50] whose characteristics it finally brings all together. This is a new point of contact that Mr. Saisset himself will be careful not to revoke in doubt, he who recognizes the perfect resemblance between the Idea of Extension and the soul of the world of Plato and the Alexandrians. That he be silent about the soul of the Kabbalists cannot be on his part a definitive exclusion; and his good faith and his science will have no difficulty in recognizing that having to choose between the Greek origin and the Hebrew origin of Spinoza's ideas, we must not stick to the first, especially since Spinoza himself refers to the second, indeed in a way to stress his own originality, both when he speaks of the truths seen by the Hebrews as through a cloud and when he mentions the traditions disfigured in a thousand ways whose true meaning he claims to expose.

No doubt, a first reading of Spinoza, a superficial consideration of his Idea of Extension is far from presenting the traits of resemblance that a deeper examination offers us with the soul of the world of Plato, the Alexandrians, the Kabbalists. Nothing, at first glance, more incompatible, more unsympathetic than the speculations of the Mystics and the demonstrations of Spinoza; and I too was hesitant to bend to the evidence that forced me to see it as a serious and original resemblance. And so I wondered:

where does this misleading impression come from that prevents us from seeing first in Spinoza what really resembles these theories of the East? Where does this astonishment come from, from which you cannot defend yourself, when you hear for the first time Mr. Saisset observe in such a frank and bold manner a kinship, a resemblance that seems to contradict the more essential characteristics of Spinoza's philosophy? No one, as far as I know, has proposed this question, and no one has solved it in a clearer and more likely way than Bayle did in the *Critical Dictionary*. Firstly, Bayle never doubted that in Spinoza's Idea of Extension was hidden the soul of the world of the ancients, and he saw by this side Spinoza touching the Stoics, that is to say the sect that Joseph Flavius did not hesitate to bring closer to his friends the Pharisees, whose dogmas had in our opinion so much part in the formation of the philosophy of Spinoza. Bayle glimpsed everywhere the Pharisaic origin of certain dogmas of Spinoza, through the Stoic mirror where they reflected from all antiquity.

And what did he see? He too saw the soul of the world, as we have just said. And answering in advance to the question we were asking ourselves just now, to the utterly extrinsic repugnance that separates the two philosophies, he gives us the most natural and satisfactory solution:

> The dogma of the soul of the world, which was so common among the ancients and which was the main part of the system of the Stoics, is basically that of Spinoza. This would appear more clearly if geometric authors (such as Spinoza) had explained it; but since the writings in which it is mentioned are more related to the method of

rhetoricians than to the method of dogmatists, and that on the contrary Spinoza has attached himself to precision without using figurative language, which so often robs us of the right ideas of a body of doctrine, it follows that we find several crucial differences between his system and that of the soul of the world.[51]

Bayle's remark cannot be overly meditated upon. It reveals in him this fine tact, this deep instinct for criticism that penetrates into the most hidden bowels of a system; it gives us the key to many enigmas in Spinoza, and it sheds great light even on the other connections we have tried between the Kabbalists and Spinoza; or, if the evidence is only the result of assiduous work and examination, it is, as Bayle says, because Spinoza attached himself to precision without using figurative language, while it is the imprecision and figurative language that characterize his models and his predecessors.

We end with this important remark, which, as can be seen, embraces all the work we have done and what we could still do. We could pursue this parallel between Spinoza and the Kabbalists in all the developments of both systems. World and Man would provide us with great and valuable arguments to better establish this Hebrew kinship that seems indubitable in Spinoza. His very theology, which has so far only been touched upon, would be much more fruitful in valuable teachings, if we could consult it more comfortably. However, the most salient points of this theology have been submitted for examination, and the result, I dare hope, has not been too unfavorable to us. Substance and its attributes, Thought and Extension, the infinity of its other unknown attributes; the Idea of God, the Idea of Thought, the Idea of Extension, have found an echo, or rather have shown themselves to be the echo of an older and no less eloquent voice. If the echo does not exactly reproduce the timbre of that voice, it is, above all, because it is only an echo, and because Kabbalah has sung its dogmas, while Spinoza has demonstrated them; it is because Kabbalist dogma is a religion, and that of Spinoza is only a philosophy, which perhaps believes itself to be of a worse kind than it really is; it is because Kabbalah is a powerful harmony, a continual hymn, and the other is only a tissue of definitions, axioms, propositions, corollaries, scholies; it is because the first has revealed its thoughts in the manner of poets, with their free gaits, their impulses and their boldness, and the second has expressed them in the manner of geometers.

A last word about the purpose of this work. We have seen Spinoza coming in almost everything closer to his predecessors, the Kabbalists; in everything, except a single point, where an abyss separates them, and this is precisely where Spinoza places Extension in his first triad in God himself, where, by a complete reversal of the Kabbalistic series, he puts Ideality at the bottom and Reality at the top; where, by a singular displacement, Extension occupies the place where the Idea of Extension should be. We have already noted this profound divergence; its importance cannot be sufficiently appreciated, because it is nothing less than the line, and what a line! that forever separates Kabbalah from Pantheism. [xxvi]

----

xxvi. When Spinoza places the Idea of God and the Idea of Thought below God and Thought, he is faithful to his system

What do we learn from this convergence on one side and this divergence on the other?

By the first, we wanted to do justice to a system that gave birth to Spinoza and his system — I am mistaken: of which Spinozism is but a mere aberration.

By the second, we wanted to signal to the friends of Spinozism on the one hand, to the opponents of Kabbalah on the other, that it would be strangely abusing a great resemblance to completely identify the two systems, and to allow oneself of Kabbalah

---

and also to Kabbalah because with regard to God and Thought, the idea of both is only a lower degree, a greater limitation, a lessening of being, a lesser reality in the ontological sense of the word. Is it the same for the Extension and its Idea? No, definitely not. Here, the Idea is greater than the Extension, because far from being a narrowing, a limitation of the Extension, it pushes it on the contrary as far as it can go: it gives it the infinity that it does not have by itself. God and Thought are circumscribed by their idea; the Extension, on the contrary, circumscribes its idea, or rather the true, eternal, infinite Extension, is only the Idea of the Extension. Spinoza believed that the idea of the two attributes of God, Thought and Extension, having the same character, must therefore suffer the same fate and this is his capital error, the misstep that made him slip into Pantheism. He saw neither the difference nor the cause of this difference; he did not see that the Idea of Extension, unlike the Idea of Thought, is larger than its object, and he did not see the cause, that is to say that the Idea belonging to Thought, and by its eminently representative character, was the source of eternity and infinity, and communicated existence to the Extension by making it thinkable, and therefore that it was the Idea itself, and not the Extension, that should take precedence in the series of emanations. Moreover, the Idea of Extension embraces Extension and not vice versa. So how could Extension precede its Idea and the content precede its container? Extension, however great it is supposed to be, will always be enclosed in its Idea, it will always be a limitation of it, and therefore must be placed below and not above its Idea.

to justify Spinoza; and that it would be a mistake no less deplorable, an injustice no less glaring, than to reject and condemn Kabbalah, on the pretext that it is only the Pantheism of Spinoza.

We will say the latter: No, Kabbalah is not Spinoza's Pantheism. It is more and better than that: it is its witness, its judge and its indictment.

Rabbi Elijah BENAMOZEGH

Editor's Endnotes

[For the *Letters*, the author gives the number of Saisset's first French edition; we give the number of the *Opera Posthuma* and the number of the van Vloten & Land 1882's edition which has become standard.]

1.   Émile Saisset (1814-1863) is the philosopher who first made Spinoza's entire *Works* available to the french reading public (*Œuvres de Spinoza traduites par Émile Saisset, avec une introduction critique*, 1842). In 1860 he published *Introduction critique aux œuvres de Spinoza*, and in 1862 *Précurseurs et disciples de Descartes*, with a detailed chapter about "Spinoza et la philosophie des Juifs".

2.   Spinoza, *Espitolae*, LXXIV. *Quod autem addis de communi hominum myriadum consensu deque interrupta ecclesiae successione etc., ipsissima Pharisaeorum cantilena est. Hi namque non minori confidentia, quam ecclesiae Romanae addicti testium myriadas exhibent, qui aequali ac Romanorum testes pertinacia audita, tanquam ab ipsis experta, referunt. Stirpem deinde suam ad Adamum usque proferunt. Eorum ecclesiam in hunc usque diem propagatam, immotam et solidam invito hostili ethnicorum et Christianorum odio permanere, pari arrogantia iactant. Antiquitate omnium maxime defenduntur. Traditiones ab ipso Deo acceptas, seque solos verbum Dei scriptum et non scriptum servare, uno ore clamant. Omnes haereses ex iis exiisse, ipsos autem constantes aliquot annorum millia absque ullo imperio cogente, sed sola superstitionis efficacia mansisse, negare nemo potest. Miracula, quae narrant, delassare valent mille loquaces. Sed quo sese maxime efferunt, est, quod longe plures, quam ulla natio, martyres numerent et numerum quotidie augeant eorum, qui pro fide, quam profitentur, singulari animi constantia passi sunt; neque hoc mendacio. Ipse enim inter alios quendam Iudam, quem fidum appellant, novi, qui in mediis flammis, quum iam mortuus crederetur, hymnum, qui incipit:* Tibi Deus animam meam offero, *canere incepit et in medio canto exspiravit.* (Letter 76, to Burgh.)

3.   Spinoza, *Tractatus theologico-politicus*, Caput VII. *Quod porro Pharisaeorum traditionem attinet, jam supra diximus, eam sibi non constare; pontificum autem romanorum authoritatem luculentiori testimonio indigere; et nulla alia de causa hanc reprobo. Nam si ex ipsa Scriptura eam nobis aeque certo ostendere, ad Judaeorum pontifices olim poterant, nihil me moveret, quod inter romanos pontifices reperti fuerint haeretici et impii; cum olim inter Hebraeorum pontifices etiam reperti fuerint haeretici et impii, qui sinistris mediis pontificatum adepit sunt, penes quos tamen ex Scripturae mandato summa erat potestas legem interpretandi.*

4.   Spinoza, *Espitolae*, XXIX (20. April. 1663).*Verum hic obiter adhuc notari velim, quod Peripatetici recentiores, ut quidem puto, male intellexerunt demonstrationem veterum, qua ostendere nitebantur Dei existentiam. Nam, ut ipsam apud Iudaeum quendam, Rab Ghasdai vocatum, reperio, sic sonat: "Si datur progressus causarum in infinitum, erunt omnia, quae sunt, etiam causata. Atque nulli, quod causatum est, competit, vi suae naturae necessario existere. Ergo nihil est in natura, ad cuius essentiam pertinet necessario existere. Sed hoc est absurdum: ergo et illud."*(Letter 12, to Meyer.)

5.   Spinoza, *Ethica*, Pars secunda, propositio VII, scholium. *Sic etiam modus extensionis et idea illius modi una eademque est res sed duobus modis expressa, quod quidam Hebræorum quasi per nebulam vidisse videntur, qui scilicet statuunt Deum, Dei intellectum resque ab ipso intellectas unum et idem esse.*

6.   דעת יודע וידוע

7.   שכל משכיל ומושכל

8.   ספר סופר סיפור

9.   כתר

10.   בינה

11.   חכמה

12.   י

13.   ה

14.   מלכות

15.   עטרת

16.   Spinoza, *Espitolae*, XXI (ad Oldenburgio , nov. 1675). *Sed, ut de tribus illis capitibus, quae notas, mentem meam tibi aperiam, dico, et quidem ad primum, me de Deo et natura sententiam fovere longe diversam ab ea, quam neoterici Christiani defendere solent. Deum enim rerum omnium causam immanentem, ut aiunt, non vero transeuntem statuo. Omnia, inquam, in Deo esse et in Deo moveri cum Paulo affirmo, et forte etiam cum omnibus antiquis*

*philosophis, licet alio modo; et auderem etiam dicere, cum antiquis
omnibus Hebraeis, quantum ex quibusdam traditionibus, tametsi
multis modis adulteratis, coniicere licet.* (Letter 73)

17.   Spinoza, *Ethica*, Pars secunda, propositio VII, scholium.
*Hic antequam ulterius pergamus, revocandum nobis in memoriam
est id quod supra ostendimus nempe quod quicquid ab infinito
intellectu percipi potest tanquam substantiæ essentiam constituens,
id omne ad unicam tantum substantiam pertinet et consequenter
quod substantia cogitans et substantia extensa una eadem que est
substantia quæ jam sub hoc jam sub illo attributo comprehenditur.
Sic etiam modus extensionis et idea illius modi una eademque est
res sed duobus modis expressa, quod quidam Hebræorum quasi per
nebulam vidisse videntur, qui scilicet statuunt Deum, Dei intellectum
resque ab ipso intellectas unum et idem esse. Exempli gratia circulus
in natura existens et idea circuli existentis quæ etiam in Deo est, una
eademque est res quæ per diversa attributa explicatur et ideo sive
naturam sub attributo extensionis sive sub attributo cogitationis
sive sub alio quocunque concipiamus, unum eundemque ordinem
sive unam eandemque causarum connexionem hoc est easdem res
invicem sequi reperiemus.*

"Before going any further, I wish to recall to mind what
has been pointed out above — namely, that whatsoever can be
perceived by the infinite intellect as constituting the essence of
substance, belongs altogether only to one substance: consequently,
substance thinking and substance extended are one and the
same substance, comprehended now through one attribute, now
through the other. So, also, a mode of extension and the idea
of that mode are one and the same thing, though expressed in
two ways. This truth seems to have been dimly recognized by
those Jews who maintained that God, God's intellect, and the
things understood by God are identical. For instance, a circle
existing in nature, and the idea of a circle existing, which is also
in God, are one and the same thing displayed through different
attributes. Thus, whether we conceive nature under the attribute
of extension, or under the attribute of thought, or under any
other attribute, we shall find the same order, or one and the same
chain of causes—that is, the same things following in either case."
(Translation Robert Harvey Monro Elwes.)

18.   מזל

19.   רצון

20.   רעוא דרעוין

21.   מקום אתרא

22.   Spinoza, *Espitolae*, LXXII (15. Iulii 1676). *Quod petis, an ex solo extensionis conceptu rerum varietas a priori possit demonstrari, credo me iam satis clare ostendisse, id impossibile esse; ideoque materiam a Cartesio male definiri per extensionem; sed eam necessario debere explicari per attributum, quod aeternam et infinitam essentiam exprimat. Sed de his forsan aliquando, si vita suppetit, clarius tecum agam. Nam huc usque nihil de his ordine disponere mihi licuit.*

"With regard to your question as to whether the variety of things can be demonstrated *a priori* solely from the conception of Extension, I think I have already made it quite clear that this is impossible. That is why Descartes is wrong in defining matter through Extension; it must necessarily be explicated through an attribute which expresses an eternal and infinite essence. But perhaps, if I live long enough, I shall some time discuss this with you more clearly; for as yet I have not had the opportunity to arrange in due order anything on this subject." (Translation Samuel Shirley, *Spinoza Complete Works*, Hackett Publishing, Indianapolis, 2002, Letter 83, p. 958.)

23.   דרור

24.   מדות

25.   Spinoza, *Ethica*, Pars prima, propositio x, scholium. *Ex his apparet quod quamvis duo attributa realiter distincta concipiantur hoc est unum sine ope alterius, non possumus tamen inde concludere ipsa dua entia sive duas diversas substantias constituere; id enim est de natura substantiæ ut unumquodque ejus attributorum per se concipiatur quandoquidem omnia quæ habet attributa, simul in ipsa semper fuerunt nec unum ab alio produci potuit sed unumquodque realitatem sive esse substantiæ exprimit. Longe ergo abest ut absurdum sit uni substantiæ plura attributa tribuere; quin nihil in natura clarius quam quod unumquodque ens sub aliquo attributo debeat concipi et quo plus realitatis aut esse habeat eo plura attributa quæ et necessitatem sive æternitatem et infinitatem exprimunt, habeat et consequenter nihil etiam clarius quam quod ens absolute infinitum necessario sit definiendum (ut definitione 6 tradidimus) ens quod constat infinitis attributis quorum unumquodque æternam et infinitam certam essentiam exprimit. Si quis autem jam quærit ex quo ergo signo diversitatem substantiarum poterimus dignoscere, legat sequentes propositiones, quæ ostendunt in rerum natura non nisi unicam substantiam existere eamque absolute infinitam esse, quapropter id signum frustra quæreretur.*

"It is thus evident that, though two attributes are, in fact, conceived as distinct —that is, one without the help of the other— yet we cannot, therefore, conclude that they constitute two entities, or two different substances. For it is the nature of substance that each of its attributes is conceived through itself, inasmuch as all the attributes it has have always existed simultaneously in it, and none could be produced by any other; but each expresses the reality or being of substance. It is, then, far from an absurdity to ascribe several attributes to one substance: for nothing in nature is more clear than that each and every entity must be conceived under some attribute, and that its reality or being is in proportion to the number of its attributes expressing necessity or eternity and infinity. Consequently it is abundantly clear, that an absolutely infinite being must necessarily be defined as consisting in infinite attributes, each of which expresses a certain eternal and infinite essence. If anyone now ask, by what sign shall he be able to distinguish different substances, let him read the following propositions, which show that there is but one substance in the universe, and that it is absolutely infinite, wherefore such a sign would be sought in vain." (Translation Robert Harvey Monro Elwes.)

26.   בריאה יצירה עשיה

27.   תפארת

28.   Spinoza, *Ethica*, Pars prima, propositio XXXI, demonstratio. *Per intellectum enim (ut per se notum) non intelligimus absolutam cogitationem sed certum tantum modum cogitandi, qui modus ab aliis scilicet cupiditate, amore, etc. differt adeoque (per definitionem 5) per absolutam cogitationem concipi debet nempe (per propositionem 15 et definitionem 6) per aliquod Dei attributum quod æternam et infinitam cogitationis essentiam exprimit, ita concipi debet ut sine ipso nec esse nec concipi possit ac propterea (per scholium propositionis 29) ad Naturam naturatam, non vero naturantem referri debet ut etiam reliqui modi cogitandi. Q.E.D*

"By the intellect we do not (obviously) mean absolute thought, but only a certain mode of thinking, differing from other modes, such as love, desire, etc., and therefore (Def. v.) requiring to be conceived through absolute thought. It must (by Prop. xv. and Def. vi.), through some attribute of God which expresses the eternal and infinite essence of thought, be so conceived, that without such attribute it could neither be nor be conceived. It must therefore be referred to nature passive rather than to

nature active, as must also the other modes of thinking. Q.E.D."
(Translation Robert Harvey Monro Elwes.)

29.   Spinoza, *Ethica*, Pars secunda, propositio IV. *Idea Dei ex qua infinita infinitis modis sequuntur, unica tantum esse potest.*

30.   In the demonstration of proposition IV.

Spinoza, *Ethica*, Pars secunda, propositio IV, demonstratio. *Intellectus infinitus nihil præter Dei attributa ejusque affectiones comprehendit (per propositionem 30 partis I). Atqui Deus est unicus (per corollarium I propositionis 14 partis I). Ergo idea Dei ex qua infinita infinitis modis sequuntur, unica tantum esse potest. Q.E.D*

"Infinite intellect comprehends nothing save the attributes of God and his modifications (Part I., Prop. xxx.). Now God is one (Part I., Prop. xIV., Coroll.). Therefore the idea of God, wherefrom an infinite number of things follow in infinite ways, can only be one. Q.E.D." (Translation Robert Harvey Monro Elwes.)

Spinoza, *Ethica*, Pars prima, propositio xxx. *Intellectus actu finitus aut actu infinitus Dei attributa Deique affectiones comprehendere debet et nihil aliud.*

"Intellect, in function finite, or in function infinite, must comprehend the attributes of God and the modifications of God, and nothing else." (translation Robert Harvey Monro Elwes)

31.   Spinoza, *Ethica*, Pars prima, propositio xxxI, demonstratio. *Voluntas certus tantum cogitandi modus est sicuti intellectus.*

"Will is only a particular mode of thinking, like intellect." (Translation Robert Harvey Monro Elwes.)

32.   Spinoza, *Espitolae*, LXVI (29. Iulii 1675). *Denique exempla, quae petis, primi generis sunt in cogitatione intellectus absolute infinitus, in extensione autem motus et quies; secundi autem facies totius universi, quae quamvis infinitis modis variet, manet tamen semper eadem, de quo vide schol. lemmatis 7. ante prop. 14. ethic. part. 2.*

"Lastly, the examples you ask for of the first kind are: in the case of thought, absolutely infinite intellect; in the case of extension, motion and rest. An example of the second kind is the face of the whole universe, which, although varying in infinite ways, yet remains always the same. See Scholium to Lemma 7 preceding Prop. 14, 11." (Translation Samuel Shirley, *Spinoza Complete Works*, Hackett Publishing, Indianapolis, 2002, Letter 64 [in fact written to Schuller], p. 958.)

33.   Émile Saisset, *Introduction critique aux œuvres de Spinoza*, Charpentier Éditeur, Paris, 1860, p. 85. "On croit

généralement que, dans la doctrine de Spinoza, entre Dieu pris en soi et les êtres finis et mobiles qui composent l'univers, il n'y a d'autre intermédiaire que les attributs infinis d'où émanent les modes, et qui émanent eux-mêmes de la Substance. Ce préjugé est une grave erreur, et j'ose dire que quiconque l'a dans l'esprit ne se forme pas une idée complète des spéculations de Spinoza. "

34. *Ibid.*, p. 86. "(...) modes d'une nature toute différente, éternels, infinis, plus étroitement liés que les âmes et les corps à la Substance. "

35. *Ibid.* "Spinoza distingue expressément deux sortes de modes éternels et infinis de la substance divine : ceux qui découlent de la nature absolue d'un attribut de Dieu, et il donne pour exemple l'idée de Dieu ; et au-dessous de ces modes, ceux qui en découlent, et qui se trouvent ainsi séparés de la Substance par deux intermédiaires, l'attribut et le mode immédiat de l'attribut. Spinoza, dans l'Éthique, ne donne aucun exemple de cette seconde espèce de modes éternels et infinis, et sur ce point grave et délicat on est presque réduit à des conjectures."

36. Spinoza, *Ethica*, Pars prima, propositio xxi. *Omnia quæ ex absoluta natura alicujus attributi Dei sequuntur, semper et infinita existere debuerunt sive per idem attributum æterna et infinita sunt.*

"All things which follow from the absolute nature of any attribute of God must always exist and be infinite, or, in other words, are eternal and infinite through the said attribute." (Translation Robert Harvey Monro Elwes.)

37. Spinoza, *Espitolae*, lxv (25. Iulii 1675). *Prioris generis cogitatio ac extensio, posterioris vero intellectus in cogitatione, motus in extensione esse videntur.*

"It seems to me that thought and extension are of the first kind, and of the latter kind, intellect in thought and motion in extension, etc." (Translation Samuel Shirley, *Spinoza Complete Works*, Hackett Publishing, Indianapolis, 2002, Letter 63 [in fact written by Schuller], p. 917.)

38. See above, note 32.

39. Émile Saisset, *o. c.*, p. 64. "La pensée divine comprend-elle aussi les attributs de la Substance? c'est un des points les plus obscurs de la métaphysique de Spinoza."

40. Spinoza, *Ethica*, Pars secunda, propositio vii, scholium. *(...) consequenter quod substantia cogitans et substantia extensa una eademque est substantia quæ jam sub hoc jam sub illo attributo comprehenditur.*

"(...) consequently, substance thinking and substance extended are one and the same substance, comprehended now through one attribute, now through the other." (Translation Robert Harvey Monro Elwes.)

41. משפט תורה

42. אחד

43. Spinoza, *Espitolae*, XXI (Nov. 1675). *Denique, ut de tertio etiam capite mentem meam clarius aperiam, dico, ad salutem non esse omnino necesse, Christum secundum carnem noscere; sed de aeterno illo filio Dei, hoc est, Dei aeterna sapientia, quae sese in omnibus rebus, et maxime in mente humana, et omnium maxime in Christo Iesu manifestavit, longe aliter sentiendum. Nam nemo absque hac ad statum beatitudinis potest pervenire, utpote quae sola docet, quid verum et falsum, bonum et malum sit. Et quia, uti dixi, haec sapientia per Iesum Christum maxime manifestata fuit, ideo ipsius discipuli eandem, quatenus ab ipso ipsis fuit revelata, praedicaverunt, seseque spiritu illo Christi supra reliquos gloriari posse ostenderunt. Ceterum quod quaedam ecclesiae his addunt, quod Deus naturam humanam assumpserit, monui expresse, me quid dicant nescire; imo, ut verum fatear, non minus absurde mihi loqui videntur, quam si quis mihi diceret, quod circulus naturam quadrati induerit.*

"Finally, to disclose my meaning more clearly on the third head, I say that for salvation it is not altogether necessary to know Christ according to the flesh; but with regard to the eternal son of God, that is, God's eternal wisdom, which has manifested itself in all things and chiefly in the human mind, and most of all in Christ Jesus, a very different view must be taken. For without this no one can attain to a state of blessedness, since this alone teaches what is true and false, good and evil. And since, as I have said, this wisdom has been manifested most of all through Jesus Christ, his disciples have preached it as far as he revealed it to them, and have shown themselves able to glory above all others in that spirit of Christ. As to the additional teaching of certain Churches, that God took upon himself human nature, I have expressly indicated that I do not understand what they say. Indeed, to tell the truth, they seem to me to speak no less absurdly than one who might tell me that a circle has taken on the nature of a square." (Translation Samuel Shirley, *Spinoza Complete Works*, Hackett Publishing, Indianapolis, 2002, Letter 73, p. 942.)

44.   Spinoza, *Ethica*, Pars quarta, propositio LXVIII, scholium. *Atque hoc et alia quæ jam demonstravimus, videntur a Mose significari in illa primi hominis historia (…) et libertatem suam amittere quam Patriarchæ postea recuperaverunt ducti spiritu Christi hoc est Dei idea a qua sola pendet ut homo liber sit et ut bonum quod sibi cupit, reliquis hominibus cupiat, ut supra (per propositionem 37 hujus) demonstravimus.*

"This, and other matters which we have already proved, seem to have been signified by Moses in the history of the first man. (…) this freedom was afterwards recovered by the patriarchs, led by the spirit of Christ ; that is, by the idea of God, whereon alone it depends, that man may be free, and desire for others the good which he desires for himself, as we have shown above (IV. XXXVII.)." (Translation Robert Harvey Monro Elwes.)

45.   שכינה

46.   Émile Saisset, *o. c.*, p. 89. "Outre l'idée de l'Étendue, nous connaissons encore une autre idée, c'est l'idée de la Pensée. Il doit y avoir, en effet, dans l'idée de Dieu, l'idée de tous les attributs de Dieu, et la Pensée est un de ces attributs."

"Besides the idea of Extension, we know yet another idea, the idea of Thought. There must be, in fact, in the idea of God, the idea of all the attributes of God, and Thought is one of these attributes."

47.   *Ibid.*, p. 87. "Maintenant, de l'idée de Dieu, qui émane immédiatement de la pensée divine, Spinoza fait immédiatement émaner certaines modifications également éternelles et infinies; et je crois entrer dans son sens en citant pour exemple, l'idée de l'étendue de Dieu."

48.   *Ibid.*, p. 89. "(…) l'idée de l'Étendue, est une émanation immédiate de l'idée de Dieu, comme l'idée de Dieu est une émanation immédiate de la pensée de Dieu (…)"

49.   *Ibid.*, p. 90. "Maintenant que contient chacune de ces idées de chacun des attributs de Dieu, par exemple, l'idée de l'Étendue? elle comprend les idées de toutes les modalités de l'Étendue. Or qu'est-ce qu'une modalité de l'Étendue? c'est une âme, une âme particulière jointe à un corps particulier. L'idée de l'Étendue enveloppe donc toutes les âmes ; elle est donc, à la lettre, l'âme du monde corporel. C'est une âme universelle, conçue à la façon des Alexandrins, dont toutes les âmes particulières sont des émanations. C'est un océan infini d'âmes et

d'idées. Chaque idée, chaque âme est un fleuve de cet océan ; chaque pensée en est un flot."

50. נפש

51. Bayle, *Dictionnaire critique*, art. SPINOZA. "Le dogme de l'âme du monde, qui a été si commun parmi les anciens, et qui faisait la partie principale du système des stoïciens, est dans le fond celui de Spinoza. Cela paraîtrait plus clairement si des auteurs géomètres l'avaient expliqué; mais comme les écrits où il en est fait mention tiennent plus de la méthode des rhétoriciens que de la méthode dogmatique; et qu'au contraire Spinoza s'est attaché à la précision, sans se servir du langage figuré qui nous dérobe si souvent les idées justes d'un corps de doctrine, de là vient que nous trouvons plusieurs différences capitales entre son système et celui de l'âme du monde."

WORKS OF ELIJAH BENAMOZEGH

אימת מפגיע [EMAT MAFGIA] (THE FEAR OF THE OPPONENT) — a refutation of Leon of Modena's attacks upon the Kabbalah, in 2 vols., Livorno, 1858.

גר צדק [GER TZEDEK] (A RIGHTEOUS PROSELYTE) — critical notes on the Targum Onkelos, Livorno, 1858.

נר לדוד [NER LE-DAVID] (LAMP OF DAVID) — commentary on the Psalms, published together with the text, Livorno, 1858.

אם למקרא [EM LA-MIKRA] (MATRIX OF SCRIPTURE) — commentary on the Pentateuch containing critical, philological, archaeological, and scientific notes on the dogmas, history, laws, and customs of the ancient peoples, published together with the text under the title תורת ה' [Torat Adonai], Livorno and Paris, 1862–65.

טעם לש"ד [TA'AM LESHAD] — refutation of Samuel David Luzzatto's dialogue on the Kabbalah, Livorno, 1863.

מבוא לתורה שבעל פה [MAVO LETORAH SHEBEALPEH] — general introduction to the Oral Tradition, published in הלבנון [haLevanon], 1864, pp. 73 et seq.

STORIA DEGLI ESSENI — Florence, 1865

צורי גלעד [TZORI GIL'AD] — response to the Rabbis of Aleppo, in כבוד הלבנון [Kevod ha-Levanon], VIII (1871), n° 43, p. 352.

MORALE JUIVE ET MORALE CHRÉTIENNE. EXAMEN COMPARATIF SUIVI DE QUELQUES RÉFLEXIONS SUR LES PRINCIPES DE L'ISLAMISME — Paris, 1867 ; (*Jewish and Christian Ethics with a Criticism on Mahomedism*, English translation by E. Blochman, 1873).

Di Dio. Teologia Dogmatica e Apologetica — Benamozegh's great theological treatise, founded on a metaphysical understanding of Kabbala, Livorno, 1877.

Le Crime de la Guerre Dénoncé à L'Humanité — Paris, 1881.

יענה באש [Ya'aneh be-Esh] (He Will Answer Through Fire) — discussion of cremation according to the Bible and the Talmud, Livorno, 1886.

Lettere dirette a S. D. Luzatto da Elia Benamozegh — Livorno, 1890.

"Gli attributi di Dio" — unpublished part of the *Teologia*, published posthumously in the journal *Lux*, 1, 190., p. 26.

Israël et l'Humanité (Israel and Humanity) — discussion of universal religion and the roles of and relationships between Judaism, Christianity, and Islam, posthumous, edited by Aimé Pallière, Paris, 1914.

La Kabbale et l'origine des dogmes chrétiens (kabbalah and the origin of christian dogmas) — written in 1860-1863, published posthumously, Paris, 2011.

Selected Bibliography

On Kabbalah's influence on Spinoza

AANEN, Johan — "The Kabbalistic Sources of Spinoza," *The Journal of Jewish Thought and Philosophy*, 24/2, 2016, 279-99.

AMOROSO, Leonardo — *Scintille Ebraiche*, Pisa: Edizioni ETS, 2004, 123-36.

BELTRÁN, Miquel — *The Influence of Abraham Cohen de Herrera's Kabbalah on Spinoza's Metaphysics*, Leiden: Brill, 2016.

BRANN, Henry Walter — "Spinoza and the Kabbalah," in Siegfried Hessing (ed.), *Speculum Spinozanum. 1677-1977*, London: Routledge & Kegan Paul, 1977, 108-18.

DUNIN BORKOWSKI, Stanislaus Von — 'Kabbalistische Wanderfahrten', *Der junge de Spinoza, Leben und Werdegang im Lichte der Weltphilosophie*, Münster i. W. : Aschendorff, 1910.

GELBHAUS, Sigmund — *Die Metaphysik der Ethik Spinozas im Quellenlichte der Kabbala*, Wien-Brünn: Max Hickel, 1917.

LEIBNIZ — *Animadversiones ad Joh. Georg. Wachteri librum de recondita Hebræorum philosophia*, first published in French translation by Louis-Alexandre Foucher de Careil in *Réfutation inédite de Spinoza par Leibniz*, Paris, 1854.

MIESES, Israel — *Spinoza und die Kabbala*, Leipzig: Louis Pernitzsch, 1869.

SACCARO DEL BUFFA, Giuseppa — "Abraham Cohen Herrera et le jeune Spinoza — entre Kabbale et scolastique: À propos de la création *ex nihilo*", *Archives de Philosophie*, 51, 1988, 55-73.

SUTCLIFFE, Adam — *Judaism and Enlightenment*, New York: Cambridge University Press, 2003, 155-156.

SCHOLEM, Gershom — 'Einleitung' to *Das Buch Shaar ha-Shamayim oder Pforte des Himmels*, Francfort: Suhrkamp, 1974; Introduction published in an augmented version in hebrew, אברהם כהן הירירה וס' שער השמים, חייו, יצירתו והשפעתה (*Abraham Cohen Herrera and his book The Gate of Heaven, his life and works and their influence*), Jerusalem: Mossad Bialik, 1978.

WACHTER, Johann Georg — *Der Spinozismus im Jüdenthumb*, 1699.

— *Elucidarius cabalisticus, sive reconditae Hebraeorum philosophiae brevis et succincta recensio*, 1706.

ON ELIJAH BENAMOZEGH

AMIR, Yehoyada — "New Paths Towards Christianity and Islam in the Thought of Nachman Krochmal and Elijah Benamozegh," in *Die Entdeckung des Christentums in der Wissenschaft des Judentums*, ed. Görge Hasselhoff, Berlin: De Gruyter, 2010, 227–38.

BOULOUQUE, Clémence — *Elia Benamozegh (1823–1900): Kabbalah, Tradition, and the Challenges of Interfaith Encounters*, Diss. New York University, 2014.

— *Another Modernity: Elia Benamozegh's Jewish Universalism*, Stanford University Press 2020.

CASSUTO MORSELLI, Marco & MAESTRI, Gabriella — *Elia Benamozegh Nostro Contemporaneo*, Genova: Marietti, 2017.

FAUR, José — "The Hebrew Species Concept and the Origin of Evolution: R. Benamozegh's Response to Darwin," *La rassegna mensile di Israel*, 63/3, 1997, 43-66.

GUETTA, Alessandro — "Un kabbaliste à l'heure du progrès: le cas d'Élie Benamozegh," *Revue de l'histoire des religions*, 208/4, 1991, 415-36.

— "Qabbalà e Cristianesimo nella filosofia di Elia Benamozegh," *La rassegna mensile di Israel*, 63/3, 1997, 21-8.

— *Philosophie et Cabbale. Essai sur la Pensée d'Elie Benamozegh*, Paris: L'Harmattan, 1998.

— *Per Benamozegh. Atti del Convegno Internazionale sull'opera di Elia Benamozegh*, Milan: Thàlassa De Pas, 2001.

— *Philosophy and Kabbalah: Elijah Benamozegh and the Reconciliation of Western Thought and Jewish Esotericism. Revised and Augmented English Version*, Collection « Contemporary Jewish Thought », Albany: State University of New York (SUNY) Press, 2009.

HAREL, Yaron — "The Edict to Destroy Em Lamikra – Aleppo 1865" (Hebrew), *Hebrew Union College Annual*, 64, 1993, XXVII-XXXVI.

HOLZMAN, Gitit — "Universalism and Nationalism, Jews and Gentiles in the Thought of Elijah Benamozegh" (Hebrew), *Pe'amim: Studies in Oriental Jewry*, 74, 1998, 104-30.

IDEL, Moshe — "Kabbalah in Elijah Benamozegh's Thought" (Hebrew), *Pe'amim: Studies in Oriental Jewry*, 74, 1998, 87-96.

KRAUS, Clara — "Elementi Di Una Religione Universale Nell'Ebraismo Secondo 'Israël et l'Humanité" di Elia Benamozegh," *La rassegna mensile di Israel*, 22/2, 1956, 65–71.

SEIDLER, Meir — "A Nineteenth Century Jewish Attempt at Integrativeness: Rabbi Eliahu Benamozegh's Multicultural Approach to Polytheism," *Yosef Da'at; Studies in Modern Jewish History in Honor of Yosef Salmon*, ed. Yossi Goldstein, Beer Sheva: Ben-Gurion University of the Negev Press, 2010, 11-23.

ZINI, Eliahu — "Due Maestri del Nostro Tempo: I Rabbini Elia Benamozegh e Avraham Itzhak Hacohen Kuk," *La rassegna mensile di Israel*, 63/3, 1997, 67-78.